MW01034028

View from the Top
of the Grand Supercycle

View from the Top
of the Grand Supercycle

Printed in the United States of America

For information, address the publishers:
New Classics Library
Post Office Box 1618
Gainesville, Georgia 30503 USA
Phone: 800-336-1618, 770-536-0309
Fax: 770-536-2514

Web site: www.elliottwave.com
More books: www.elliottwave.com/books
E-mail address for products:customerservice@elliottwave.com
E-mail address for comments: bb@elliottwave.com

New Classics Library is the book-publishing division of
Elliott Wave International, Inc.

ISBN: 0932750559
Library of Congress Control Number: 2002108348

View from the Top
of the Grand Supercycle

Robert R. Prechter, Jr.

New Classics Library

*This book is dedicated to our loyal subscribers,
who stay with us through think and thin
because they "get it."*

Acknowledgments

I would like to thank the writers whose contributions enhanced this book. Thanks also to the proofreaders, who suggested well-needed minor edits. Finally, I would like to acknowledge the contributions of Rachel Webb and Sally Webb, who handled production, and Darrell King and Robin Machcinski, who designed the dust jacket.

Table of Contents

Publisher's Note.. xi

***Section One*:**   **Key Essays on the Topping Process of
the Great Asset Mania**

Leading Up to the Peak of the Average Stock in April 1998

May 1997   Bulls, Bears and Manias.. 4

June 1997   Why the Market is in An Extended Fifth Primary
Wave, Not An Extended Third............................. 22

August 1997   The High-Yield Index... 25

March 1998   Style of the Bear Market.. 26

March 1998   A Confluence of Fibonacci Time Spans................. 28

April 1998   The Nostradamus of Wall Street............................ 34

April 1998   The Millennium... 43

April 1998   Relax?... 45

Leading Up to the Peak in the Dow in January 2000

September 1998   A Major Deflation Is Approaching......................... 48

September 1998   The Decoupling Arrives.. 52

Nov/Dec 1998   Elliott Wave Investing... 58

December 1998   A Peek at the Future... 62

February 1999   Game Over... 65

July 1999   Technical Analysis Profile: Robert Prechter........... 68

July 1999   You Heard It Here First... 74

December 1999   An Overview of the Long Term Elliott Wave
Case for Stocks.. 75

Battling Euphoria in the Post-Peak Topping Process

February 2000   Part 1: Questions & Answers With Bob Prechter   92
Part 2: Fibonacci Relationships in Cycle Wave V   99

February 2000   Deflation and the New Economy............................105

April 2000	Letter to the Editor	116
May 2000	Deflation and Real Estate	118
May 2000	One Small Step for the Utilities	120
July 2000	Rationalizing High Stock Valuations	123
July 2000	"All We Need..."	124
July 2000	A Major Stock Market Low is Still Due in 2003-2004	125
August 2000	"New Economy" Fever	136
August 2000	Bust Just Ahead?	137
October 2000	GE 1974-2000 = *phi* x 100	140
December 2000	The Economy	142

Section Two: **Retrospective: Errors Made and Knowledge Gained**

	Perspective	145
	Calling Too Many Tops	149
	Why I Was Early and What We Have Learned	164

Postscript

	Timer Digest Cover Story	185
	Long Term Forecast Still in Progress	188

Publisher's Note

The greatest prize sought by a wave analyst is to identify a stock market juncture at the highest possible degree. To date, the largest turns identified in print have been of Cycle degree: a bottom in 1942 by R.N. Elliott, a top in 1966 by Charles Collins and a bottom in 1974 by A.J. Frost. (For the full story, see *R.N. Elliott's Masterworks, The Complete Elliott Wave Writings of A. Hamilton Bolton* and *The Elliott Wave Writings of A.J. Frost and Richard Russell*.) It may be argued that at the 1942 and 1982 lows respectively, Elliott and Prechter identified Supercycle degree turns in inflation-adjusted terms (see Figure A-1 in the Appendix to *Elliott Wave Principle*). The long term tops in gold, silver and the rate of inflation that Prechter called for in December 1979 (see Chapter 14 in *At the Crest*) were also of Supercycle degree, judging from the two decades of decline that they have since undergone. The opportunity to experience the termination of a *Grand* Supercycle degree advance in the stock market, however, arises perhaps only half a dozen times in a millennium. In the era of Elliott knowledge, it has yet to happen until now.

It would seem proper to have the whole world standing by to watch as electronic postings of the main stock averages reach top tick right down to the one-minute chart. Such an event is impossible, of course, as it would mean that people's unconscious herding impulse had been fully integrated into their conscious understanding, in which case humanity would have conquered waves, so they wouldn't exist. Don't expect that to happen any time soon. To those who understand what is going on, though, it seems a travesty that so few care to pay attention.

Prechter's first bearish message to the public, *At the Crest of the Tidal Wave* (1995), forecasted approaching major tops in about a dozen financial markets. It was early, as the top in the global bull market for stocks has taken some time to play out. The Southeast Asian markets fell in 1997. In the U.S., the total number of new one-year highs on the NYSE peaked in October 1997. The Value Line geometric stock index and the advance-decline line, which represent most stocks, turned down in April 1998. The Dow and the S&P valued in real terms — i.e., vs. commodities and gold — topped in July 1999. (See Chapter 18 in the second edition of *Market Analy-*

sis for the New Millennium.) The nominal stock indexes for the U.S. and Europe continued higher until early 2000. In the meantime, bond quality has been slipping ominously while real estate has continued to rise selectively, suggesting a maturing multi-decade bull market.

In a sense, this volume is an extension of the analysis in *At the Crest*, presenting major Elliott wave essays from *The Elliott Wave Theorist* and its companion publication, *The Elliott Wave Financial Forecast*, that have accompanied the topping process in the U.S. stock market from 1997 through 2000. This is not a full record of our authors' ongoing commentary on all markets covered, which would fill ten times the space. We are publishing these essays simply to show that in the face of unbridled public and professional adoration for stocks, Prechter and company have waged a heroic battle against the dizzying peak and post-peak euphoria and remained steadfast in calling for a top and reversal of historic proportion.

In section two of this book, Prechter candidly reviews reasons why he turned bearish too early on the U.S. stock indexes and sheds new light on how Elliott waves behave in an investment mania. We suspect that Elliotticians will be studying this section for years to come.

This book includes some rare media coverage and interviews with Prechter during this period. They are rare because in the past few years, the media have been bullishly biased to a 99.9 percent ratio of its "talking heads" and uninterested in profiling a bearish outlook. Sure, bears have been wrong for awhile, but in market forecasting, as in sports, there is no such thing as 100 percent pass completions or batting averages of 1000. For the media to ignore one side or the other because it has recently been wrong is to assure that the correct voice will never be heard at the turns. What good is that? As an antidote, we at New Classics Library like to provide the missing voice, whether bullish or bearish.

Most publishers issue bullish books late in a bull market and bearish books late in a bear market. This is a great way to sell books by the truckload, but it doesn't help investors; it hurts them. We take a different tack. Our bullish book — *Elliott Wave Principle*, which Prechter wrote with A.J. Frost — came out in late 1978, at a stock market bottom. Naturally, it couldn't compete with the scary tomes on the bestseller list, but it was worth a fortune to those who read it. Our bearish book came out seventeen years later. Similarly, it couldn't compete with the flood of bullish books pouring off the presses, but it has provided value to those who read it by getting them to sell their investment assets into strength at historic overvaluations.

Perhaps this dichotomy is as it should be. According to Plutarch's *Lives*, after the Athenian general Phocion received enthusiastic applause for his remarks to a crowd, he turned to an associate and asked, "Have I said something foolish?" Playing to the crowd, as most publishers do, does not require wisdom so much as craft. At New Classics Library, we hope to err on the side of wisdom. Subscribers had the advantage of reading these essays in current time, but even retrospectively, *View from the Top*, we contend, will prove more useful today than yet another "Stocks to the Moon" book. It is coming out in time to *help you* while the Dow is still near its high. Although we suspect that this book will have few readers, we hope it finds its way to you somehow anyway.

After reviewing the final edits for this book, Prechter recalled a favorite tag line of the late climatologist, Iben Browning, who used to conclude his speeches by saying, "I may be wrong, but I haven't been casual." That's the way we feel about our books.

Section One
KEY ESSAYS ON THE
TOPPING PROCESS OF
THE GREAT ASSET MANIA

Leading Up to the Peak of the Average Stock in April 1998

The Elliott Wave Theorist
Special Report

May 21, 1997

Bulls, Bears and Manias

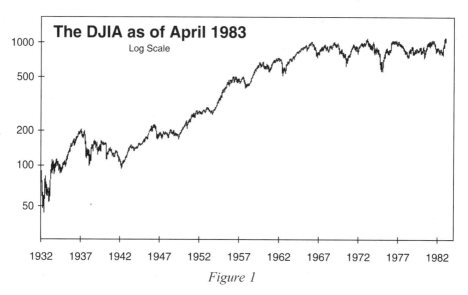

Figure 1

"*Finally, given the technical situation, what might we conclude about the psychological aspects of wave V? The 1920s bull market was a fifth wave of a <u>third</u> Supercycle wave, while Cycle wave V is the fifth wave of a <u>fifth</u> Supercycle wave. Thus, as the last hurrah, it should be characterized at its end by an almost unbelievable institutional mania for stocks and a public mania for stock index futures, stock options, and options on futures. In my opinion, the long term sentiment gauges will give off major trend sell signals two or three years before the final top, and the market will just keep on going. In order for the Dow to reach the heights expected by the year 1987 or 1990, and in order to set up the U.S. stock market to experience the greatest crash in its history, which, according to the Wave Principle, is due to follow wave V, investor mass psychology should reach manic proportions, with elements of 1929, 1968 and 1973 all operating together and, at the end, to an even greater extreme.*"

    —The Elliott Wave Theorist, "A Rising Tide," April 6, 1983

Typically, bull and bear markets flow into one another. A bull begets a bear, and vice versa. At rare times in history, each of these may have an exceptional offspring.

For a bear market, the exceptional offspring is a decline to worthlessness. Instead of a bull market emerging where it typically would, the bear market accelerates and carries to oblivion. An example might be the financial and social decline that took place in Rome in the 400s. No bull market followed; it was the end of the market itself.

For a bull market, the exceptional offspring is a mania. That is, instead of a bear market emerging where it typically would, the market recovers and carries to the stratosphere. If the difference in the two phases of rising prices were only quantitative, there would be no real difference; one would simply discuss degree. But there is a *qualitative* difference between a bull market and a mania. A mania is not simply a "big bull market." It is something else, and it not only behaves differently, but it *resolves* differently as well, which is why the difference is worth knowing.

Normal market behavior is the result of a chaotic feedback system, which produces a fractal movement. As long as the society involved is viable, the long term direction of the stock market remains up, but it is interrupted by setbacks of various sizes. The frequency of those sizes is roughly proportional to the time between them; i.e., roughly speaking, 1% setbacks happen weekly, 15% setbacks happen annually, 50% setbacks happen twice a century, and so on. As long as the market exhibits this "breathing" phenomenon, it is healthy. Take a look at Figure 1, the DJIA from 1932 to 1982. Notice the irregular yet fractally patterned beat: rally is followed by correction, bull market is followed by bear market, and long rising phase is followed by long non-rising phase. The same behavior held sway from 1857 to 1921. When the market abandons this style, something else is going on.

The first aspect of a mania is that it produces a *powerful, persistent rise with remarkably fewer, briefer and/or smaller setbacks*. In studying such times in market history, we find that manias typically involve *broad participation by the public* and end at times of *historic overvaluation* by all traditional measures. These three aspects of manias are well-known by financial historians. Other aspects are not so well-known. One is that they are *born of long term bull markets*, which is to say that every mania is preceded by a long period of oft-corrected rising prices. When the time is right, the public begins to acquire the understanding that "the long term trend is always up" and increasingly acts as if, and ultimately presumes that, *every* degree of trend is always up.

When is the time right for this mindset? Simply stated, it is right when the market enters a fifth wave advance of Supercycle or larger degree. Demonstrating that this claim is not made in retrospect, the quotation that begins this paper stands as the only example in history of a mania being *forecast*. Most people do not even recognize manias as such when they are in them (which is why they are possible). The Wave Principle provides the only way to *anticipate* manias, which are exceptionally few and far between. Forecasting fifth waves is covered in several Elliott Wave books. Our limited purpose here is to describe the unique characteristics of a mania for the purpose of confirming that one is in force now, and more important, to display what typically follows for the purpose of forecasting what will happen *afterward*.

To that end are shown here pictures of five market events: the Tulip Mania culminating in 1637, the South Sea Bubble of 1719-1720, the Roaring 'Twenties stock advance of 1921-1929, the Value Line index run-up in 1966-1968 and the leap in collectible coin prices in the late 1980s. The first three of these were bona fide manias. The rise in the Value Line index was not a mania, but it is the closest thing to a mania that a large number of people alive today personally experienced, which is why I show it. While it had some of the typical aspects of a mania in mild form, it was not a one-way market. As you can see, there were significant corrections along the way. (This advance was a fifth wave of only a Cycle degree bull market, which is why it displayed moderate mania-like behavior; in the DJIA, it was a bear market rally.)

The rapid gain in coin prices displayed in Figure 6 had all the characteristics but one: It lacked broad public participation. The buying was done by brokerage firms in *anticipation* of public demand, which never actually materialized! The resulting picture is exactly the same, however.

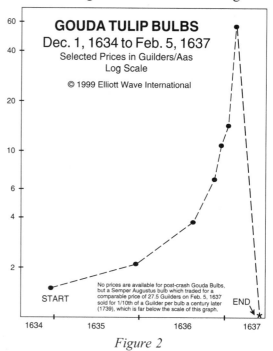

Figure 2

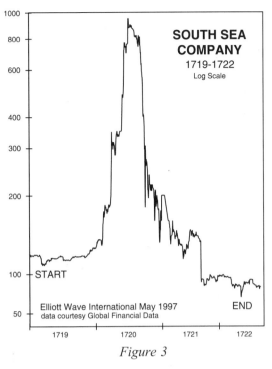

Figure 3

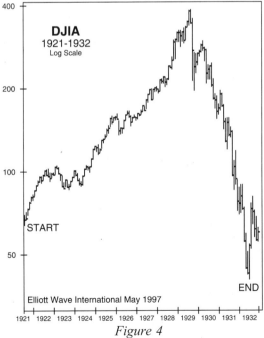

Figure 4

Figure 5

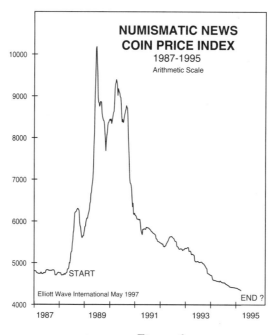

Figure 6

The Aftermath

Webster's *Third New International Dictionary* defines "mania" in the individual as an "excitement of psychotic proportions manifested by mental and physical hyperactivity, disorganization of behavior, and elevation of mood." This is highly descriptive of its social manifestation as well. It is worth noting that the word more specifically refers to "the manic phase of manic-*depressive* psychosis." Is there a social parallel to the latter half of this experience, too? Apparently so, as a consistent element in these pictures brings us to this most important observation about the market's action following a mania: *Regardless of extent, every mania leads to a decline that ends below the starting point of the advance.*

Considering the heights that manias reach, this is an amazing fact. Tulip bulb prices had been substantial for years and then soared in 1634-1637, reaching thousands of guilders (see Figure 2). Just one year later, city councils in Holland passed regulations allowing tulip bulb futures contracts (yes, they were a "sophisticated, modern" financial society, too) to be paid off at 3.5% of the contract price. A footnote in the book *Crashes and Panics* by Eugene N. White adds that the decline in prices was probably greater than 96.5% because many of these contracts were not fulfilled even at that price. A few decades later, a bulb could be had for 10 cents. In other words, these "investments" declined in value nearly 100%. The collapse following the South Sea Bubble (see Figure 3) also ended below its starting point. In fact, of all the stocks listed on the London exchange at the peak, only 9% remained two years later. Taking into account the stocks that went to zero, the average issue declined 98% in less than two years. The 1920s advance in the Dow Jones Industrial Average (see Figure 4) began at the 64 level, while the ensuing 89% decline brought the average down to 41 in less than three years. At the top, over 800 issues routinely traded every day on the New York Stock Exchange. Three years later, it was half that number. By 1933, many companies, municipalities and even some mutual funds had failed. The substantial public participation in the stock rise of 1966-1968 (see Figure 5) was enough to condemn the gains to more than complete retracement as well, as the Value Line index thereafter fell 74% in six years. Again with coin prices in the late 1980s (see Figure 6), had an investor been clever enough to buy just *before* the explosive advance, he would currently have a loss.

Why must a mania be *more* than fully retraced? Fifth waves in the stock market are sometimes fully retraced, but often not. Socially speaking, we might surmise that because in a mania so much of the public pins its hopes for the future on the market, the decline that follows is not simply a bear market correcting the excesses of the investment community, but an all-encompassing event that destroys many people's fortunes, which in turn had supported the economic success of the society.

The scientific explanation, I expect, has to do with the disruption of a properly functioning chaotic system. Here is a quote from "Science Watch" in *The New York Times* of April 15, 1997:

> "Dr. Ary L. Goldberger, director of electrocardiology at Beth Israel [hospital], determined that healthy hearts exhibit slight *fractal-like irregularities* — patterned variations of beating. A heart beat that seems *abnormally smooth and free of fractal variations may actually signal an impending heart attack.*" [ellipsis omitted; emphasis added]

The same thing, I submit, is true of investment markets. When they become smoothly-trending and free of fractal variations, they depict an unhealthy patient and signal an impending "heart attack."

To introduce another analogy, manic markets are akin to people abusing "speed." In foregoing sleep, amphetamine abusers disrupt the healthy ebb and flow of consciousness that is required for healthy long term functioning, just as manias disrupt the ebb and flow of prices that is required for healthy long-term advance. Like manias, amphetamine abusers perform abnormally well for awhile...until they crash. When they crash, they reach a state worse than the one they were in when they began the abuse, just as a market does after a mania. In each case, a long period of convalescence and recovery is required.

Closer To Home: The Nikkei Through 1989

Figure 7 is the Japanese Nikkei stock index from the 1940s to the present. This market had all the aspects of a mania, in spades. If the aftermath of this one is true to form, then the decline that began on the first day of 1990 is not over. It will have to carry below the starting point of the mania. In this case, that level is somewhat debatable, but I conservatively date its start as October 1974. That is when bull markets ceased alternating with bear markets and the one-way climb began. The low that year was 3355, so the Nikkei should be on its way to below that level.

Figures 7 through 10 show this and the U.S. market on both arithmetic and logarithmic (percentage) scale. All manias accelerate in arithmetic terms, and most do so at some point in percentage terms as well, as U.S. stocks did in 1928 and again recently, post-1994.

The decline from the 1989 high in the Nikkei looks more or less normal on log scale (see Figure 8). Why isn't it just a bear market that corrected the preceding excesses? The 1929 crash in the U.S. (see Figure 4) was perceived exactly that way by most investors, which is why trading volume in the post-crash bear market rally exceeded that of the all-time high. However, the key to understanding the meaning of these declines is the all-important fact that they *followed a mania.* The first large decline afterward signals a major reversal, not simply a "correction." The 1929 crash of 48% was nothing compared to the stair-step collapse that followed, beginning in April 1930, and it is likely that the Nikkei's 63% drop of 1990-1992 will be seen retrospectively in the same light.

The U.S. Investment Mania: Greatest of All Time?

Starting in 1982, the U.S. stock averages (see Figures 9 & 10) have exhibited all four signs of a mania: emergence following decades of oft-corrected rising prices (and a price plateau, as in the 1920s), wide public participation, brief and minimal corrections, and historic overvaluation. There are four reasons to rank it among the greatest manias of all time, possibly *the* greatest.

First is the fact that it has an unprecedented depth of participation. In the U.S., public involvement in the market has probably set a record for any nation in history. Two polls report that 43% of households have a direct or indirect (through corporate pension plans) stake in the stock market. At over 40%, the share of households' financial assets that are *in* stocks is the greatest ever as well. [These figures later exceeded 60% and 46% respectively. —Ed.] Indeed, the mania for stocks is global, including even the former and current bastions of communism.

Second is the duration of the mania. This is the main reason I turned bearish way too soon, despite my own description 14 years ago of what the investment environment would be. Other manias have lasted far less time. The tulip mania lasted three years, the South Sea Bubble two years. The rises in the Value Line index and the coin market shown here lasted only two years. The longest recorded mania had been the 1920s' eight-year rise. Based on wave relationships in normal bull markets and the 1920s experience, *The Elliott Wave Theorist* in 1982-1983 forecasted either a 5-year or 8-year advance, to peak in 1987 or 1990. While these years marked near-term tops, they did not see the end of the mania. Indeed, from a psychological standpoint, it was just getting started. The Japanese experience

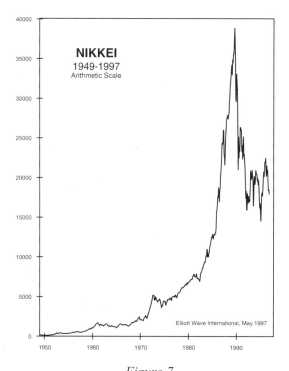

Figure 7

Figure 8

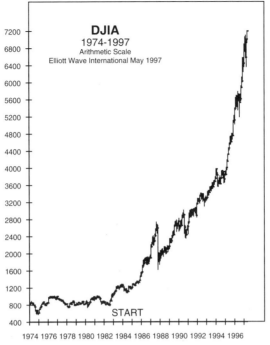

Figure 9

Figure 10

has lengthened the historical record for manias, to 15 years, from 1974 to 1989. Now the U.S. stock mania, which began in August 1982, is approaching 15 years in length.

Third is the extent of the mania. In September 1982, *The Elliott Wave Theorist* called for the Dow to rise 5 times in value to 3885, a level that appeared absurdly high. With respect to manias, it was actually not that high. The 1920s rise was a 6-times multiple. The South Sea Bubble was an 8-times multiple. Well, the Dow passed even that historic milestone when it exceeded 6215! The only recorded manias that were greater were the Nikkei, an 11-times multiple in fifteen years, and the tulip mania, an estimated 40-times multiple in three years. The Dow today is nearly double my original forecasted high and will match the Nikkei rise of 11.089x if it reaches a daily close of 8615. Beyond that will make it the biggest *stock* mania of all time, leaving only the infamous tulip mania as a contender for the highest title of this millennium.

Fourth, this mania has something very rare: *official sanction.* Two of the greatest manias of recorded history, the South Sea Bubble in England and the Mississippi Scheme in France, both of 1720, were initiated by government action. From an Elliott Wave standpoint, the current mania is ending a two-century advance, the same "Grand Supercycle" degree rise that ended with the South Sea Bubble, which is why I forecasted a mania in the first place. Perhaps manias of this degree induce official sanction, which in turn helps to stimulate excesses of this degree. While the government did not initiate today's mania, there is no question that it has *supported* it. Alan Greenspan, chairman of the Federal Reserve Board, a quasi-government agency (despite its official description), specifically stated on January 14, "We have the responsibility to prevent major financial market disruptions through the development and enforcement of prudent regulatory standards and, if necessary in rare circumstances, through direct intervention in market events." Indeed, the start of the runaway phase of the current mania emerged after the market's digestion of the rumor that the Fed had intervened in the stock market on October 20, 1987 to stop the panic. No U.S. agency had ever done that before. It put stock investing in a new light. The mighty Fed had exhibited a vested interest in stopping declines, a fact that was not lost on the psyche of investors. In the same spirit, Congress and the Securities and Exchange Commission have repealed or relaxed numerous laws and rules governing investment that had been in place since the 1930s (in response to the aftermath of the *last* mania). In recent months, the Social Security Administration has expressed interest in buying stocks to keep the government's retirement-guarantee system from going bankrupt. National officials and agencies have thus placed their stamp of approval on the advance, a powerful psychological deterrent to caution and thus to normal market behavior.

Fifth, today's investment mania is far broader than past manias, at least as far as I can discern from a cursory reading of history. It is certainly not limited to stocks. In the past decade, almost anything that can pass for an asset has been fair game for a bidding war:

Real estate. Almost every area of the country has experienced a real estate bubble some time in recent years. In 1989, people in California camped out all night in a long line for the chance to outbid each other on a house.

Bonds, where lack of quality is no object. The worldwide bond mania has encompassed such low-grade issues that a new word was coined to reflect them: "junk." Some issues, described in *The Elliott Wave Theorist*, appear guaranteed to fail, yet have been snapped up by investors.

Coins. (See Figure 6.)

Art. In 1989, a single painting (Van Gogh's "Irises") sold for $89 million. This month, a Warhol "Soup Can" (of which the artist produced at least two dozen, according to a source) sold for $3.5 million.

Baseball cards. In the 1980s, collectors became "investors" and shops opened everywhere, as card ownership became a mania. Stock investors bid up card manufacturer Topps Co., then sold it mercilessly when the mania ended.

Jackie Onassis' back-of-the-closet junk. For example, one of President Kennedy's sets of golf clubs sold for $772,500, which was 96,463% above Sotheby's pre-auction estimate of $800.

Dolls. In 1987, Cabbage Patch Kids had become so desirable and overpriced in the aftermarket that some people flew to England to buy them when U.S. stores ran out. Last Christmas, Tickle-Me-Elmo dolls became a craze and sold for as much as $10,000 when stores ran out. In 1997, even kids talk about how a "rare" version of the suddenly popular Beanie Babies stuffed animals can fetch $1500 among "investors," even as the manufacturer continues to pump them out as fast as it can.

"Classic" cars, vinyl records, meteorites, pop culture memorabilia, you-name-it.

Even within the overall stock mania, there have been mini-manias. Biotech stocks soared in 1991, "emerging" overseas markets in 1992-1993, Internet and penny mining stocks in 1995-1996. Bre-X Minerals Limited climbed from about 18 cents to $28, then collapsed when revealed to be a fraud. Comparator Systems went from approximately 3 cents to $1.78 in four days in May 1996 before collapsing for the same reason. Computer chip stocks have had an intense focus for almost two years. There are countless others, and the list is growing. Is this the greatest investment mania of all time? Probably. If it ends as manias have in the past, then prices on every item listed above will eventually fall below its lowest price of the 1980s-1990s.

The Top

It has been demonstrated quite thoroughly that I am unable to predict the end of a mania. Maybe the market will produce a strong sign at its end, and maybe it won't. One of the most interesting aspects of the charts shown herein is the fact that *unlike typical bull markets*, manias do not undergo much in the way of "distribution." They end on a dime, and the trend changes.

Some signs do occur in advance of the turn. In the 1920s, the advance-decline line fell for a year before the top. This dry technical indicator reflected a very real experience, as noted by Col. Leonard Ayres of the Cleveland Trust Co., who said this in 1929:

> "This has been a highly selective market. It has made new high records for volume of trading, and most of the stock averages have moved up during considerable periods of time with a rapidity never before equaled. Nevertheless, the majority of issues had been drifting down for a long time. In a real sense, there has been under way during most of this year a sort of creeping bear market."

In 1929, "secondary," or lower-priced and lower-capitalized, stocks lagged while selected blue chips roared. The same phenomenon occurred preceding the major market tops of 1937 and 1973. Thus, such behavior took place just prior to the three biggest stock declines of this century. As with the Nikkei, whose a-d line declined throughout its manic period, the a-d lines for the NASDAQ and S&P indexes saw their highs in 1983 and 1989 respectively, 14 and 8 years ago! (The NYSE a-d line has continued to rise, but for the first time in history, it is no longer representative of common stock behavior. The New York Stock Exchange includes many bond-related issues and mutual funds, which go up when the averages go up, even if only a handful of stocks propel them.) The divergence in behavior between blue chips and secondaries has become noticeably extreme in recent months, as the Russell 2000 index of small-cap stocks has lagged the S&P 500 significantly since May 1996. The difference is so great that *The Wall Street Journal* reports on May 7 that for the second time in a row, its semi-annual "contest" between professional stock-pickers and "dart-throwers" resulted in losses for *both*. The four professionals lost an average 13.6%; the dart-throwers lost an average 9.7%. Absent other information, you would think a bear market has been in force. However, the DJIA climbed 15.3% during that period. The WSJ calls that rise "healthy" and concludes, "Here's another reason to like index funds." In fact, this situation is historically *un*healthy. The increasingly selective mania will ultimately include the indexes among its casualties.

One sign of the top that appeared in 1929 was a deceleration of the advance in its final year. Unfortunately, the 1920s advance decelerated several times prior to the top, just as this one has, so while a top may follow deceleration, deceleration does not ensure an approaching top.

Perhaps the U.S. stock mania will closely match the Japanese experience with a 15-year duration. There is no reason, however, why this one *cannot* set a new record. Manias are not bounded on the upside by quantitative criteria.

The Approaching Resolution

The difference between a normal bull market and a mania is crucial to understand because the great price rise in U.S. stocks since 1982 will not be followed by a proportional "bear market" that corrects only the run-up from 1982. It will yield to a *more than complete retracement* as part of a correction of the entire advance from the late 1700s. Of course, Elliott Wave analysis has indicated this outcome from the start. Our 1978 book, *Elliott Wave Principle*, which forecasted the great wave V advance, also said that it would be followed by a decline in the DJIA into the area of the "preceding fourth wave of one lesser degree," which is the 1920s advance. Since then, *The Elliott Wave Theorist* has simply stated the ultimate target as "below 400." The very idea of such a decline appears as lunacy, a fact to which I am sensitive due to the scorn it invites, despite which I am not deterred. If anything, the history of manias depicted here shows that it remains a sensible conclusion. The fuel for this extraordinary event will be monetary deflation, as outlined in *At the Crest of the Tidal Wave*.

The Insidiousness of a Mania

Historians characterize a mania as a kind of madness that takes hold of a population. The widely shared illusion of endless huge profits that propels a mania also produces another kind of madness: anger. Though the media report new highs in the averages with a giddy demeanor, it is a clown mask that hides a miserable soul.

A very human aspect of manias is that no prudent professional is perceived to add value to a client's investment experience. Indeed, the professional with a knowledge of history and value is eventually judged an impediment to success. The reason is that the investments that are the focus of the mania are widely accepted as the *benchmark of normalcy*. Therefore, only a professional who "beats" that benchmark is considered successful. As the focus of the mania narrows, that task becomes impossible. This is yet another difference between a normal bull market and a mania. In a bull market, professionals can add value relative to the benchmark, which is usually conservative (the short term lending rate, for instance). In a mania, no one can add value. That is the situation today.

Let's review five types of professionals who have an approach that, in competent hands, "works" in most market environments and see how they are faring today.

(1) *Market timers*: Look back at Figure 1, the DJIA from 1932 to 1982. For half a century, the stock market ebbed and flowed in such a way as to make good market timing a significant added value. Today, with the trend having gone one way for an entire decade, there has been *nothing to time*: nothing significant in the way of waves, cycles, corrections or bear markets.

(2) *Value buyers*: From 1932 to 1983, stocks that appeared undervalued by the market when priced against dividends, book value and earnings typically returned to greater valuation, providing an advantage to the investor who purchased issues meeting those criteria. The demoralizing story of this bull market for such investors is how substantially such stocks have been lagging the averages and indeed falling in recent months while the S&P soars.

(3) *Quants and "diversifiers"*: Diversification into several asset classes, regardless of the weightings, has guaranteed significant underperformance relative to the S&P.

(4) *Money managers*: Managers of money-market funds, bond funds and mixed funds have obviously underperformed the S&P. Even 100%-stock fund managers cannot keep pace. In the past year, 80% of stock mutual funds failed to outperform the S&P. So far in 1997, the figure is 96%. The reason is that the S&P itself is at the heart of the mania.

(5) *Stock brokers*: Competent brokers have had a role to play in assisting investors, but in the current environment, nothing formerly prudent works. In the past year, brokerage firm research departments have repeatedly recommended $20 stocks that go to 6. Trading customers mostly sell

short, trying to catch a pullback that is "long overdue," then join the advances too late out of desperation, losing in both directions. The firms' managed funds have gone up, but they lag the S&P.

In all these cases, the client becomes livid. "How can my market timer not see that stocks always go up?! How can this stodgy value buyer sit year after year in stocks that are stuck in the mud?! Why does my advisor have my account 40% in bonds and 10% in bills when obviously the action is in the stock market?! What's wrong with my broker? Almost everything he picks goes down! How come my fund is lagging the S&P by so much? What am I paying those guys for?! *Everybody's getting rich but me!*"

The result is that every professional who knows *bull and bear markets but not manias*, and every client thereof, is to some degree stressed and unhappy. In recent conversations, brokers have told me, "These are the worst months of my life." "My clients are getting killed." A money manager confesses, "I am chronically depressed." Market timers have few subscribers left and wonder if continuing is worth the effort and anxiety. This situation is totally different from that of a healthy bull market, where good money managers, timers, brokers and their customers are relatively happy. In a mania, those who spent a professional lifetime studying the typical ways of the market are deemed fools, and their utterly unknowledgeable novice clients tell them so, month after month. Because a mania is so psychologically powerful, the clients have become dictators to the professionals, at least to the vast majority of professionals who have succumbed. The choice is not how to play the game (as it is in a bull market), but whether to play it. Money managers who refuse to accept the market's ultimatum to become heavily invested in mania stocks lose most of their customers.

The only players who feel like (and are, temporarily) winners are index fund managers who can spell the 500 names in the S&P index, the "momentum" buyers who chase whatever stocks are racing upward, and the investors who plunge into the vortex. These people are positively euphoric, and for good reason. Month after month, indeed year after year since 1992 when the fund craze took hold, they have reaped what looks like free money, and all of it can be attributed to their guts and acumen.

Ultimately, however, a mania and its aftermath have everyone for lunch: first the bears and contrarians, then the prudent professionals relying on long-term studies, and finally the plungers who fancy themselves clever investors and pour most of their funds into the market in its final run. Even among prudent professionals who remain in business, the aftermath is no kinder than was the mania itself. A competent money manager's greatest claim on the way down will be that he is losing a lesser percentage of his clients' money than the averages, which is something the clients will not want to hear. Suddenly the "benchmark" that seemed so sensible on the way up is no longer acceptable. "The averages don't matter! Stop losing my money!" Market timers cannot provide much value on the way down, either. Post-mania declines are typically as persistent as the mania was on the way up, if not more so. There are no significant advances, no "getting even," no way to take advantage except to sell.

Surveying the scene several years after a mania has occurred, it appears fitting that Mania was an obscure ancient Roman goddess of the dead. Except for any individuals (real or mythical) who by luck or skill get in early and get out at the top, the ones who survive in the long run are those who stay in cash and do not participate.

Technical Note

I contend that major commodity price rises, while similar in profile, do not often qualify as manias. The engine of a commodity boom is usually fear (of shortage, war, inflation, etc.), not hope and greed, so the entire phenomenon is fundamentally different. Commodity booms do not necessarily follow long periods of jagged advance, either, but sometimes emerge suddenly from lengthy doldrums. Rarely is the public broadly involved, because commodities are typically not considered to be long-term investments. For instance, when the price of silver exploded upward from $4 to $50 per ounce in late 1979 and early 1980 in response to inflation fears, many people lined up outside depositories not to buy it, but to sell the family silver. This never happens in manias. Furthermore, because commodity booms do not always emerge as Supercycle and larger fifth waves of much larger structures, they are not necessarily more than fully retraced, though they are usually substantially retraced. Although one might concede that an exception to this observation is possible, the Tulip Mania is not one of them, as tulips are not staples but have an aesthetic appeal akin to art works and can therefore foster a collectible appeal.

The Elliott Wave Theorist
Special Section

June 27, 1997

Why the Market is in
an Extended Fifth Primary Wave,
Not An Extended Third

Subscribers have asked with increasing frequency about the validity of long term wave counts presented by other Elliott wave analysts who argue that the market is only now in the "third of the third" wave center of a rise that has a decade or two left in it. Take a look at Figure 1-9 from *Elliott Wave Principle*, shown on the next page. This is the picture numerous others are anticipating. Since the market has gone straight up for ten years, they conclude that it is somewhere within wave three of three, etc., portending several larger fourth and fifth waves ahead that will take years to unfold. I disagree with that conclusion for the following reasons:

It is crucial to recognize that the stock market is in a fifth wave of Cycle degree within a fifth wave of Supercycle degree. One or two analysts dispute this fact, but it is definitely the case, given (1) the excellent Elliott wave in inflation-adjusted stock values from 1784 to 1966 and (2) the deterioration in the rate of economic growth from 1932 to the present vs. that from 1857 to 1929 and again from 1974 vs. 1942-1966. These data, along with some of the points made below, argue against the idea that we have embarked on some kind of third wave of giant degree. For details, see *Elliott Wave Principle* and *At the Crest of the Tidal Wave*.

Most analysts agree with that much and simply expect Cycle *wave V* (from 1974 or 1982) to exhibit an extended third wave, as per Figure 1-9. This is the most common form in normal bull markets, as a certain Mr. Prechter pointed out in *Elliott Wave Principle* twenty years ago in contradicting R.N. Elliott's belief that extended fifth waves are more common. Assuming so in every case, however, is lazy analysis based only on average probability. Is it not necessary to investigate when the less common forms are likely? Elliott concluded that extended fifth waves were more common *because his research was conducted in the environs of a*

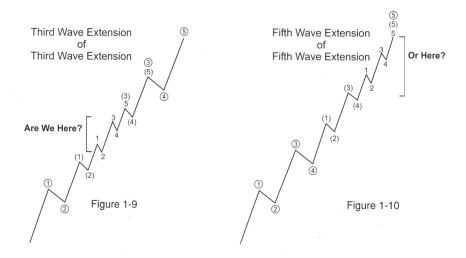

Figure 1-9

Figure 1-10

Supercycle degree top. That is exactly the environment today, and that is exactly when extended fifths are more common.

The guideline of alternation alone (see *Elliott Wave Principle*, p.61) would suggest a difference from the extended third wave of Cycle wave III from 1942 to 1966. Expecting the market to do the same thing that it did in the preceding wave of the same degree will put you in error almost by definition.

Finally, the market is in a mania. The position of the market in the largest "fifth of the fifth" wave since 1720, the minimal corrections and the historic overvaluation all confirm it. *The Elliott Wave Theorist* forecasted today's market psychology 14 years ago, so this is not a retrospective analysis but one we anticipated (and then, unfortunately, thought too soon had ended). Here is what pertains: *No mania in history has ever traced out an extended third wave and then undergone a long period of distribution.* Every one has ended suddenly, often shortly after the point of maximum acceleration, as you saw by the charts in the May Special Report, "Bulls, Bears and Manias." Nothing is impossible, but when history gives you consistent results under certain conditions, it is prudent to apply the lesson accordingly.

For these reasons, the better picture is Figure 1-10, shown at top right above. It is akin to what happened in the 1920s and a more apt description of what is happening now. The main point is that corrections will tend to get *smaller* into the top, not larger.

[*Note: The notion of an extended third wave has lasted as long as the mania, showing just how far some analysts are willing to project the uptrend. Apparently they are perfectly comfortable with the popular calls for Dow 35,000, 100,000 and higher. — Ed.*]

August 1, 1997

The High-Yield Index

Many dealers want to drop the "junk" label in favor of "high-yield." Those who remember what happened from early 1988 through 1990, however, when these bonds declined by more than 55%, will not let go of the term "junk."

As long as the default rate stays near its record low of 1.5%, a premium of 2.75% above Treasuries will remain a good deal. Given the assurance, however, that the economy will contract one of these days, we have to wonder what kind of a secondary market there will be for a $150 million casino issue and a $1 billion collateralized bond obligation.

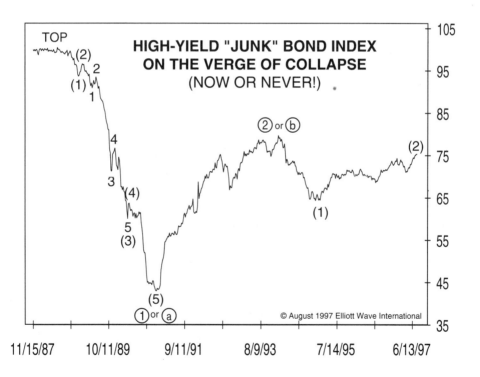

The Elliott Wave Theorist
Special Report

March 12, 1998

Style of the Bear Market

The bear markets of 1720-1722 and 1835-1842 progressed at about the same speed as the final years of their preceding bull markets. While they did not announce themselves with giant gap-down one-day crashes, neither were they slow and deceptive. They were simply *relentless*. They included numerous mini-crashes as well as short rallies, but the overall profile month after month was just plain down. The accompanying chart details the great South Sea Company stock bubble of 1719-1720, as well as its aftermath. Notice how much the right side of the chart looks like the left. Although the 1929 crash got all the headlines, the wipeout of 1930-1932 was similarly relentless and ultimately much more destructive. It was a speeded-up version of the rise from 1924 to 1929. Given all this precedent, there is substantial reason to believe that the coming bear market will be much like a reverse image of 1982-1998(?), probably speeded up.

Of additional interest to us, of course, is that the South Sea Company pattern displays impeccable "Elliott." The advance is a classic "five," right down to the 9-wave extension in wave ⑤. The bear market then began with a crash in five waves, constituting wave A of an A-B-C bear market. Wave A progressed at about the same rate as the preceding wave ⑤ rise. This pattern of five waves down is exactly what *At the Crest* (see Chapter 5, section titled "How the Pattern Will Start") forecasts for the coming bear market.

A relentless bear market at Supercycle degree will be something to behold. Given that the size of this bear market will be the largest in over two centuries, there will likely be numerous days that the press labels "crashes" that in fact are only part of the relentless downtrend, not crashes at Supercycle scale.

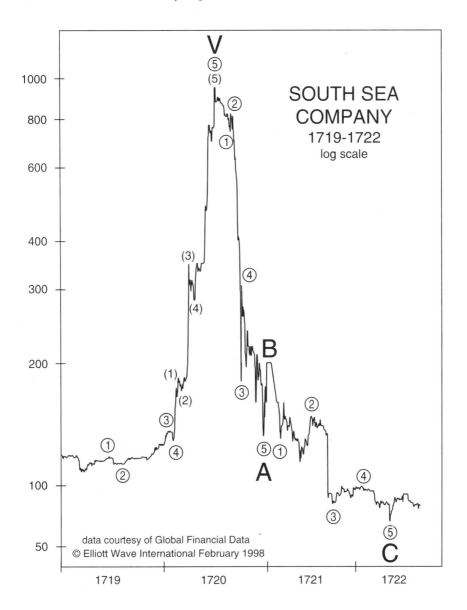

SOUTH SEA
COMPANY
1719-1722
log scale

data courtesy of Global Financial Data
© Elliott Wave International February 1998

March 27, 1998

A Confluence of Fibonacci Time Spans

Eight Fibonacci time spans, involving weeks, months and years, are culminating. As Hamilton Bolton said, such spans are not always present, but turning points in the market appear to be separated by a Fibonacci number of time units (3, 5, 8, 13, 21, 34, 55, 89, etc.) more often than chance would allow. When several of them coincide, the potential for a turn increases.

Years

Observe in Figure 1 that a Fibonacci **8** years have separated four key turning points beginning with the 1966 high of Cycle wave III: **1966, 1974, 1982** and **1990**. (1990 is a more important low than generally acknowledged, as it ended a three-year bear market in the Value Line index that began in 1987.) If that duration is to mark a fifth turning point, it will occur eight years from 1990, in **1998**.

Months

Take a look at Figure 2 and observe these three durations:
—**5** months from the October 1997 low = **March 1998**.
—**21** months from the July 1996 low = **April 1998**.
—**89** months from the October 1990 low = **March 1998**.

Weeks

Take a look at Figure 3 and observe these four durations:
—**21** weeks from the October 1997 low =
                          the week of **March 23-27, 1998**.
—**34** weeks from the August 1997 high =
                          the week of **March 30-April 3, 1998**.
—**55** weeks from the March 1997 high =
                          the week of **March 30-April 3, 1998**.
—**89** weeks from the July 1996 low =
                          the week of **March 30-April 3, 1998**.

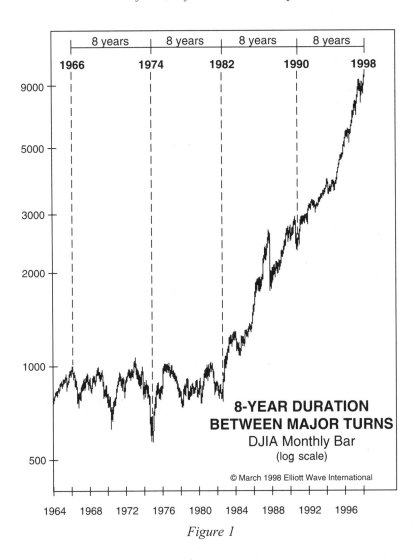

Figure 1

EWT reader Dale Woodson points out that the July 1996 low was a pivot point that led to the March 1997 high after 34 weeks and the August 1997 high after 55 weeks. This precedent should make the 89 weeks from July 1996 to now all the more reliable in marking a turn.

Time Summary Indicates a High in 1998

Observe in Figure 4 that waves I and II of the Supercycle took the same time, 5 years each. Now waves IV and V have taken the same time,

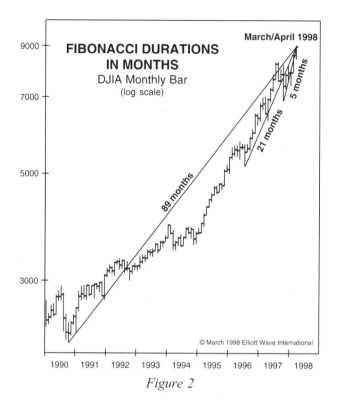

Figure 2

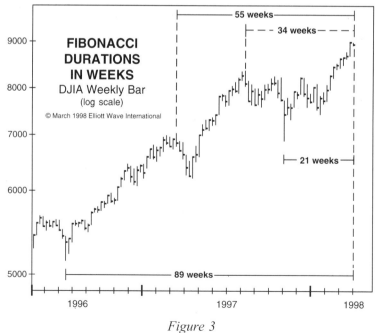

Figure 3

16 years each. So the Supercycle began and may end with time symmetry in adjacent waves. In inflation-adjusted terms (not shown), 1966-1982 is wave (A) of a Grand Supercycle correction, while the rise since 1982 is wave (B). In 1998, these two phases will have taken equal time, 16 years each. Let's not forget the 1974 low, which may be the orthodox start of wave V. The wave V rise from 1974 has lasted **24** years, the same time as the wave III rise from 1942 to 1966. From there, it has generated a **16x** (actual 16.035) multiple, which is 2.69 times the 1920s' multiple, not too far from a Fibonacci 2.62 relationship. To conclude, the market would produce many symmetries by peaking in 1998 near current levels.[1]

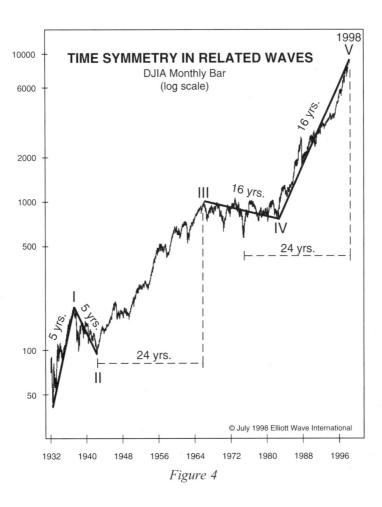

Figure 4

To summarize these influences, the monthly spans point to a market turn in March-April 1998, while the weekly spans narrow it down to **March 23-April 3**. Because the market has become, in technical parlance, "extended" on the upside, this culmination of Fibonacci time spans, if it turns out to coincide with a turn, can mark only a peak.

The last time we observed a cluster of Fibonacci time spans was 1996. It did not work out. In each case such as this, we must be alert and demand near-perfection. Allowing only one week's leeway, if the averages close higher after April 10, the implications of these durations will no longer apply. That is a tight range of time, and therein lies its value.

*[Note: Although most averages continued higher, the NYSE daily advance-decline line — and therefore the greatest number of stocks — made its all-time high on **April 3, 1998**, as you can see in Figure 5 on the next page. It has since been falling in its largest decline in 2½ decades. — Ed.]*

NOTE

[1] This observation on symmetry came from the July 10, 1998 issue.

Figure 5

Atlanta **magazine**

April 1998

The Nostradamus of Wall Street

by David Black

In the late 1980s there wasn't anybody hotter, at least in the financial world, than Robert Prechter. From his home on Lake Lanier, Prechter, then only in his mid-30s, was regularly hurling thunderbolts. An economic forecaster wielding a hard-to-grasp theory of historical trends, Prechter was proving uncannily accurate. Not only that, his forecasts were so contrary to popular opinion on Wall Street at the time, *so out there*, that he soon took on an aura of mystery. How does he do that? Soon, the financial press was wearing a path — well not a path, really, it was more like a rut — to his front door. Scoop: *He went to Yale!* Scoop: *He used to be a drummer in a rock band!* Scoop: *He holds his running shoes together with duct tape!*

In 1989 Financial News Network named him "Guru of the Decade." In retrospect, that was probably the kiss of death, because once you're a guru, what direction is left for you to go?

Cut to 1998. Prechter still lives on the shores of Lake Lanier, still makes his forecasts using the same analysis of historical trends known as the Elliott Wave Principle. But the financial press stops by like never; and when they do, they usually whack him over the head. As one swipe in *The Wall Street Journal* put it: Prechter has gone "from stock market hero to punch line of in-crowd jokes." Why? Because during the same years that the Dow Jones average has been rising over 8,000, Prechter has been consistently forecasting that the Dow is about to plunge back to 1,000 *or lower.* His extreme bearishness during this decade's bull market has gotten him tagged with a different, less flattering label: WRONG.

But in 1998, as Asian economies continue to stumble and Americans of most every demographic stripe keep shoveling money into 401(k)s and counting on a rising stock market to fund their retirements, the stakes are higher than ever before. Is it possible that the man who was a guru in the 1980s, but a nobody in the 1990s, is on track to be right again?

Ralph Elliott believed that social behavior, or crowd behavior, moves in recognizable patterns. Elliott was a successful businessman in the early part of this century — he was appointed Chief Accountant of Nicaragua in 1924 by President Calvin Coolidge's State Department — who didn't start developing his theories until after he retired in the 1930s. To test his ideas, Elliott took as his laboratory the stock market, tracking the ups and downs of investor psychology through decades, even centuries, of successive bull and bear markets. In the end, he believed he established predictable long-range behavior patterns, or waves, that would regularly occur into the future just as they had in the past.

To adherents like Prechter, the belief that these patterns of behavior — or psychological progressions — repeat themselves again and again over time is what gives Elliott's waves their predictive power.

"Mass investor psychology swings from pessimism to optimism and back in a natural sequence, creating specific patterns in price movement," Prechter has written. "Investors form a crowd whose collective action reflects a key aspect of man's nature as a social animal: He is strongly induced to adopt the feelings and convictions of the group.

"As a result, market trends are steered not by the rational decisions of individual minds, but by the peculiar collective sensibilities of the herd." Thus, "the psychological progression through each bull and bear market is always the same," regardless of the length of the trend.

Prechter discovered for himself Elliott's work in the 1970s, when he was working as a market analyst on Wall Street, and fell in love with it. In 1978 Prechter co-authored a book that extended and refined Elliott's theories and reintroduced them to the general public.

Reduced to its simplest formulation, the Elliott Wave Principle says that progress is not a straight line, but instead happens in a pattern of three steps forward and two steps back, which in turn produces trend lines that look like a slightly tilted staircase. Upward leaps in a trend line, the Dow Jones stock average for instance, are followed by slips backward, followed by another upward leap, followed by another slide backward, etc.

Practically speaking, Elliott Wave analysts like Prechter say they have identified five major bullish waves of economic behavior in the United States since 1780. Forecasting the duration of the current fifth wave — dating roughly from the end of the Great Depression — is critical, because Prechter believes the fifth wave marks the end of a grand cycle of bull markets and that exceedingly rough water will follow.

In 1978 Prechter made his first public forecast based on Elliott's theories. His prediction? A bull market of epic dimensions was on the horizon and it was time to buy stocks.

It is hard to understand how contrary such an idea was 20 years ago. It was the era of Jimmy Carter and the "national malaise;" interest rates were 20 percent; inflation hadn't yet been tamed and a second gasoline crisis was underway. The stock market had just emerged from a sustained bear market that left the Dow Jones average closer to 500 than 1,000. *Business Week* ran a cover proclaiming "The Death of Equities." Nobody wanted to know about stocks, much less own them.

The stock market did begin to rise, but very slowly. Around 1982, when the Dow was still under 1,000, Prechter forecast it would reach 3,700. He was widely ridiculed as insane, but the Dow continued to rise, reaching over 2,700 by 1987.

In 1987 Prechter made his most famous call, warning his readers in October to get out of stocks. Later in the month came Black Monday, a one-day drop of more than 500 points on the Dow. Such a spectacular short-term success finally cemented his reputation with the business media as a full-fledged guru, but also sowed the seeds of his future irrelevance.

Although almost no one remembers it now, Prechter's bull-market forecasts of the early 1980s had a second part to them that went like this: While the bull market he foresaw would be unprecedented in degree, it also would mark the end of the fifth wave and a grand cycle of economic expansion. Thus, according to Elliott Wave Principle, it would be followed by a stock market decline of similarly spectacular dimensions, "the biggest financial catastrophe since the founding of the Republic," Prechter wrote in 1983. "We had better make our fortunes now...."

Although the market quickly recovered from the 1987 crash, Prechter soon became convinced that, despite his 3,700 prediction for the Dow, the bull market was over. By the late 1980s he turned bearish, very bearish, on stocks. On this point his timing was very, very wrong. The Dow reached 3,700 in 1993 and, as the public climbed aboard the mutual fund train with their 401(k) accounts, kept rocketing upward. Despite another one-day 554-point loss in October 1997, the Dow has gone over 8,000.

Ironically, Prechter had written years earlier about the very position he now found himself in. Writing in 1983 about the bull market he foresaw, he said "turning major-trend bearish too early will be the biggest mistake you can make." In 1987 he told *The Wall Street Journal,* "I'm probably going to be wrong about something in a big way around the top.... I'll probably express caution too early, in which case people will say baloney on this crash stuff."

That prediction has turned out to be one of his best.

Today the 49-year-old Prechter, who is plain "Bob" to everyone who knows him, is, in some ways, bigger than ever, even though his media profile is almost zero.

His business, Elliott Wave International, which used to fit in the basement of his home, now employs 65, including 15 market analysts. His monthly newsletter, which peaked at around 20,000 subscribers, has dropped back to maybe 5,000 hard core fans. His readership overall, however, is much larger because his company produces five written and six on-line publications worldwide. He has expanded his advisory services into markets like commodities, currency and fixed-income analysis. Eight years ago he began a pricey advisory service for institutional investors, like insurance companies and banks, which has proved successful, too.

His friends and co-workers, many of whom have worked for him a decade or more, uniformly praise him for being "humble," "down-to-earth" and a "regular guy." Most seem in awe of his intellect and his writing ability, which is indeed a cut above most people who write about markets and money. He still eschews fancy cars (he drives a 1981 van) and fancy real estate, spending his time at Lake Lanier with his children. He still loves to play and listen to rock music, primarily 1960s bands. His all-time favorites? Quicksilver Messenger Service, Santana, Steamhammer, Francoise Hardy and anything from the British Invasion.

Prechter stopped speaking to the media and making regular public forecasts in the late 1980s. Analyzing his own career and public image at the time, he determined that, according to wave theory, he was due for a fall. Since then the trashing he has taken in print and on television has reinforced his hermitic tendencies. Today he gives almost no interviews and accepts only the rare speaking invitation. For this story he agreed to answer questions put to him by e-mail and determinedly deflected any questions that required revealing any personal information. "My family, like most people, is not used to media treatment, so I will leave them out."

These days Prechter's quest is to continue to promote the Elliott Wave Principle, not just as a tool for predicting markets, but as a way of predicting societal shifts in general. Prechter now views himself as a sociologist, and what makes him more interesting now than 10 years ago is that his ambition is so large.

"What matters to me," he says, "is establishing the fact that social systems follow certain mathematical laws, just as do physical systems.

"I disagree with the conventional wisdoms that social mood and history are random, or that they simply follow physical laws of cause and effect but are too complex to predict."

Prechter is passionate about exposing Elliott's theories to scientists working in other fields. Last year he gave a speech to an international conference of scientists in Washington and has been invited to speak at another in Israel this year. He believes advances in esoteric fields like fractal geometry and chaos theory are beginning to confirm Elliott's discoveries and that eventually they will be seen as "to the successful study of aggregate human behavior what Newton's discoveries nearly 300 years ago were to the successful study of physics."

Indeed, the Elliott Wave Principle was never intended just to solve financial riddles. The stock market just provided the best data for testing forecasts. Prechter and others have tried their hand at predicting everything from politics to hemlines to trends in music and movies. On Prechter's web site (http://www.elliottwave.com), for instance, is an essay about basketball that explores "the sport's propensity to crown the greatest teams and heroes at the most explosive points in the bull market, as well as its regression to violence and chaos in bear markets." That prediction sounds on the mark if you consider Michael Jordan, the five-time-in-the-1990s champion Chicago Bulls, and, more recently, coach-choker Latrell Sprewell.

When pressed, though, Prechter can still turn his attention to markets, although his interest now lies mainly in calling long-term trends. His opinion about the stock market today is the same as it was in 1995 (when the Dow average was 4,000-5,000), when he wrote his last book, *At the Crest of the Tidal Wave* (New Classics Library, a division of Elliott Wave International).

Says Prechter today, "The U.S. stock market is in the grip of an investment mania. A mania is a persistent uptrend that attracts the public in large numbers and leads to historic overvaluation. In the past 300 years for which data is available, no major stock market in the Western world has been as overpriced as U.S. stocks are today. The Japanese Nikkei index was valued slightly higher at its 1989 high, and it has dropped 65 percent since then. All manias end below where they started. I do not know where or when the high will be. All I am sure of is the ultimate outcome."

On the subject of the end of this bull market, consider what Prechter wrote in his newsletter in April, 1983: "What might we conclude about the psychological aspects? ...As the last hurrah, it should be characterized at its end by an almost unbelievable institutional mania for stocks and a public mania for stock index futures, stock options, and options on futures. In my opinion the long-term sentiment gauges will give off major-trend sell signals two or three years before the final top, and the market will just keep on going."

Underestimating the hunger of the public to buy stocks in the 1990s is why he has missed so badly on where the market would peak, says Prechter. "It is a perfectly justifiable gripe" to accuse him of being wrong for much of this decade, he says, but boasts he was the only forecaster to predict a future mania, "using exactly that term" in 1982-83. "That's all the defense I'm willing to play," he says.

Manias are very rare and extreme events, and have some particular characteristics. For instance, the belief that you can make money simply by buying any stock — "aggressive complacency," a horrified Prechter calls it — or the idea that buying and holding is the only successful approach to stocks, or that any market dip signals an opportunity to buy. These ideas, which are considered near-gospel in the pages of today's personal finance magazines are, to Prechter, very bearish indicators.

"People do not adopt quasi-religious attachment to stocks except when it is very late in the game," he says. "They loathe, fear and avoid them when they are a bargain. It may sound like a paradox, but it is true by definition and cannot be otherwise."

In other words, today's investors, most of whom aren't old enough to have personally experienced a bear market, simply don't know that stocks can go down as well as up. And with a public more broadly and deeply invested in stocks than ever before in history, a severe bear market could be profoundly destabilizing for the country.

Prechter's own ideas, dating back to 1983 and elaborated on in 1995, about the dimensions of such a bear market are chilling. Investors at first will buy the dips, but as the market averages keep drifting steadily downward and fortunes are lost, that advice will soon be discredited. Buy-and-hold will seem a fool's strategy. The investor who today sneers at a five percent annual return will be seen in the future as insufferably arrogant. The final resting place for the stock market? Below 1,000. In the past, Prechter has not been afraid to use the word *depression.* Investors will take to the streets and the courts looking for scapegoats; governments will be brought down. War is not out of the question. For investors there will be few places to hide. Deflation will affect almost every asset category.

Prechter dismisses ideas that this is a "new era," that the world economy has developed in a way that makes the old measurements irrelevant. "There has never been a major top in history that was not accompanied by 'new era' talk," he says. He has a similarly dim view of contemporary investment advice, which he says is simply made up of extrapolations of recent trends, "fine as long as last year's trend continues, and devastating when it doesn't."

In fact, when asked what one thing he would want people to remember about investing, his answer is bleak: "Don't do it. Unless you make it your lifelong passion, commitment and business, you will regret it."

None of this impresses Prechter's critics, of course. His cycles and ideas about market timing are dismissed as witchcraft or worse. In the financial world, missing a bull market is the greatest sin, since only the savviest professionals know how to profit from a bear market.

"You can't say that because [Prechter] has screwed up five years in a row, he has a great chance of being right next year," says Dr. Donald Ratajczak, director of Georgia State University's Economic Forecasting Center, who calls Prechter's prediction of a less-than-1,000 Dow "nonsense."

"I don't see why he talks in those terms," Ratajczak says. "A good person who uses Elliott Wave theory has to have a combination of good sense and mathematics. It sounds like all he has is mathematics and he has lost his common sense.

"I'm hard pressed to describe our market as a bubble about to burst. Overpriced? You can argue about that, but it's not a bubble."

But Prechter's is no longer a voice in the wilderness. Mainstream writers are beginning to ask hard questions about the American dependence on the stock market. In *Rolling Stone*, William Greider writes that annual real returns of 15 percent could plunge to 5 or 6 percent. "'This shift in fortunes will be dramatic and painful but need not be regarded as tragic — unless you actually believed that your little mutual-fund account was going to make you rich."

Greider says the nation's disinflation trend cannot go on much longer without threatening growth. "When prices are falling across the board, everything else must sooner or later fall, too — wages, sales, employment, profits," he writes. "As the downward spiral knocks down everything, deflation could mutate into depression."

Prechter's work is also too long-term oriented for most professionals. For them, a correct forecast is helpful, but only if it comes true within a couple weeks or months at most. Predictions that take years to come true may win grudging intellectual respect, but what broker or money manager would still be in business today if they had advised clients to sit on the sidelines of the stock market for the last seven years?

None of this worries Prechter in the least. In the Elliott Wave universe, being way, way, way out of fashion is a necessary condition to being right and being a lonely bear today reminds him of how he was a lonely bull 15-20 years ago. "One thing I have learned," he wrote in 1995, "is that if the majority does not laugh at or dismiss as worthless my long-term market opinion, it is wrong." More importantly he wants ultimate validation of Elliott Wave Principle as a predictive tool for calling long-term trend changes.

Which isn't to say there aren't professionals who find Prechter fascinating. Mark Scott runs a hedge fund in Atlanta and guest lectures for a class in technical market analysis at Georgia Tech. He remembers hearing Prechter speak three years ago. "It was like listening to Columbus saying, 'Let's assume for a moment that the world isn't flat. What then?' He's very articulate, very persuasive. He has a lot of conviction."

Scott also agrees with Prechter about the consequences of not respecting bear markets. On a recent trip through Japan, Scott asked one money manager whether he believed in buying and holding stocks like U.S. investors do. No, the investor said, the only thing Japanese investors believe in now is "sell and forget." Says Scott, "That's what five years of a bear market can do. I know that sometime in the next 20 years nobody will want to own stocks. Prechter's point is, when we get to a Japanese-type of bear market, what are you going to remember? That Prechter was wrong for five years, or that he was right on the long-term trend?"

Because his forecast is so extreme, Prechter is often accused of selling gloom-and-doom. There's no doubt that some market bears have become famous over the years — anybody remember Ravi Batra? — but, to be fair, Prechter has been both bullish and bearish over the years, and, as he notes himself, there is no market for bearish opinion today. "The way to get really rich," he says, "is to play to the crowd. Tell them what they want to hear."

But that's not Prechter's game. The Elliott Wave Principle requires the courage to stand up against the crowd. For Prechter, who "always" follows his own market advice, that means he will continue to keep his money primarily in short-term government securities and other cash equivalents, ruing the fact that he missed the second half of the biggest bull market in U.S. history, but convinced that he will be right in the long term.

Ironically, it is Prechter's record over the long term that, despite his short-term failings, makes you wonder, just a bit nervously, what if maybe, just maybe, he's right? Trouble is, by the time we find out, it will be too late.

Atlanta writer David Black is a former editor of the Atlanta Business Chronicle.

South **Magazine**

April 1998

The Millennium

Atlantans, seemingly always poised on the brink of something bigger, better and brighter, generally brim with enthusiasm over the prospects of our booming city. There's a contagious optimism in the air, a sort of wide-open-spaces bravado that gets the leadership up crowing in the morning. Los Angeles must have felt this way in the 1930s, New York in the 1920s.

But there are contrarians too, who rightfully point out the all-too-obvious stresses that could make a mess of the city's wonder years.

Every voice is valued. And many of our most distinguished speak in this landmark edition of South.

Here are 100 reflections on the coming millennium and Atlanta's place in it, from some of our most visionary minds.

Bad Moon Rising?

In 1975, when Atlanta was in recession, the Braves were in the basement and property was in a deep slump, it would have been uncommonly bold to forecast, "The next quarter-century is ours." It also would have been correct.

The 1990s have seen the flowering of Atlanta's run to glory, as the city has gained international status, hosted the Olympics, run the busiest airport, built the most mansions, won the World Series and even sent its premier college basketball team to the Final Four and football team to a national championship. These great achievements have been a joy.

However, the future is never an unbroken extension of the recent past. History is ebb and flow, and as we approach the millennium, forces are in place to cause a multi-year setback for Atlanta.

Some of Atlanta's strengths are also its areas of vulnerability. Atlanta is a financial center. The lubricant of finance is speculation, confidence and expansion. Today, the stock and bond markets, which fuel our financial industry, are overvalued and leveraged to the hilt. According to one source, the most aggressive real estate speculation in the country is right here in Atlanta.

In 1975, things looked bad, providing an excellent base upon which to build a huge expansion. In 1998, things look great, but the expansion is stretching to a limit.

Even so, the rest of the country is likely to have a similar experience, and all else being equal, wouldn't you still rather live in Atlanta than anywhere else?

Robert Prechter
President, Elliott Wave International

© 1998 *South* magazine

April 1998

Relax?

by Marc Faber

Money manager and editor of The Gloom, Boom & Doom Report

Whether it is a time for investors to "relax" or not, only time will tell. Possibly the market is, as many experts along with Abby Cohen point out, only "fairly" priced. But if this is so, after the Dow Jones Industrial Average has risen from a low of 777 in August 1982 to over 8,800 just recently (up 11 times), one has to wonder why, in the early 1980s, the same experts failed to realise how grossly undervalued U.S. equities (as well as bonds) had become. The only stock-market strategist I am aware of who, at the time, predicted a substantial advance in U.S. equity prices was Robert Prechter. In 1978, he published, with Alfred Frost, *Elliott Wave Principle* in which he predicted that the Dow Jones would rise to 2,860. In the third edition of the book, published in 1983, Prechter increased his target for the Dow Jones to a range of 3,500-4,000. Needless to say, with the Dow Jones hovering around 800 in the late 1970s, people took him about as seriously as they did Jules Verne in 1865, when he published *De la Terre a la Lune.*

In this respect, I remember one of the first conferences where I was invited to present my views on equities and bonds. It was in 1982 or 1983, and although gold had already collapsed from its 1980 high, while oil prices were trending down, the main topics of the conference were gold and gold stocks, further U.S. dollar weakness, accelerating inflation, and oil and oil stocks. My session on equities and bonds ran in the afternoon of the first day. How many participants attended my presentation? Two — one of whom left after about 10 minutes.

Leading Up to the Peak in the Dow in January 2000

Editorial submission to *The Wall Street Journal* on September 14, 1998 and to *The New York Times* on December 12, 1998

Unpublished

A Major Deflation Is Approaching

Economists are nearly unanimous in their opinion that deflation is highly unlikely. Among the handful of economists allowing for the possibility, there seems to be an equally strong consensus not only that deflation will do no harm but that in fact, it will be beneficial. "Don't worry about deflation," says a money manager on financial television, "all it does is pad profits." "Deflation," says a headline, "is nothing to fear." "History tells us," says an economic consultant, "that deflation caused principally by excess supply is a good deflation." The model for this optimism is the period from 1870 to 1897, when wholesale prices declined by half in an orderly manner. This model is inappropriate to today's situation.

First we must define deflation. Just as inflation is an expansion in the supply of money and credit, deflation is a contraction in the supply of money and credit. Deflation is *not* falling prices. Falling prices are a consequence of deflation. It is dangerous to confuse the two ideas because prices can fall without deflation. In a vibrant capitalist economy with a stable money supply, prices naturally fall as technology improves. Consumer goods prices decline as factories become more efficient; commodity prices decline as methods of extraction improve. For instance, over the past two decades, prices relating to computer hardware and software have fallen over 90% in dollar terms during a time when the U.S. money supply was consistently expanding, i.e., *despite* inflation. As an example in the area of commodities, the dollar price of oil has dropped 65% over the past two years without a contraction in the money supply. It can be highly misleading to confuse price changes with inflation or deflation.

The period from 1870 to 1897 was one of generally conservative monetary policy among bankers. There was no society-wide culture of low-reserve bank lending and no massive government borrowing to expand the money supply. Consequently, there was no net inflation. At the same time, this Gilded Age enjoyed great increases in productivity and efficiency. The result was falling prices. Deflation was not the cause and indeed was not significant. If one considers deflation possible, then he must face history and investigate the causes and consequences of a collapsing supply of money and credit.

In most cases, major deflation is a reaction to what precedes it. Its antecedent is a ballooning of the credit supply by cooperating debtors and creditors during a period of extreme financial confidence that fosters a speculative boom. Deflation followed the national property boom of the 1830s. Deflation followed the stock and real estate boom of the 1920s. Deflation followed the stock and real estate mania of the 1980s in Japan. Deflation is currently underway throughout the rest of Asia following the wholesale financial speculation of the 1990s. While there were brief periods of investment excess in the 1870s, there was no comparable nationwide financial speculation, as revealed by the stock averages of the time. The significantly milder speculation of the time preceded a significantly milder deflation.

What triggers the change from boom to deflation is a reversal of the prevailing social attitude from more financial confidence to less. When that change occurs, sellers begin to overwhelm buyers, investment prices fall, and debtors and creditors reverse their behavior, paying off and calling in loans. As a result, the credit supply contracts.

Most analysts presume that such sea changes are fostered by the mechanics of central bankers' fiscal or monetary policies, but they are primarily the product of social attitudes about lending, borrowing and risk-taking in general. Policy tinkering can (and typically does) accommodate or encourage a social attitude, but it cannot change one. The World Bank, for example, found out that it was easy to encourage a boom in Indonesia but impossible to halt the collapse that followed. Indeed, its foot on the gas pedal in the form of easy loans almost certainly contributed to the severity of the ensuing crash. Similarly, the Japanese government has discovered that despite a persistent lowering of its lending rate from near 7% to 0.5%, that country's developing deflation and depression have continued apace. The famous phrase, "pushing on a string," which refers to times when central banks cannot find takers for loans even at the easiest possible terms, speaks to the impotence of fiscal policy when risk-taking attitudes change.

Some famous economists insist that all one need do to combat deflation is print money. That may be true, but the only way that authorities will print money is if social and political attitudes encourage or permit it. That does not happen in deflations, when the increasingly conservative attitude that fostered the shift to deflation in the first place becomes even stronger.

Following forty years of accelerating inflation from 1940 to 1980, it has taken nearly two decades of monetary conservatism to bring the U.S. inflation rate from 18% to near zero. The attitude that caused that transformation will not change on a dime.

Where are we now? The U.S. is at the end of the longest inflationary period in its history by a substantial margin. The slowing rate of inflation since 1980 has fueled investor confidence so powerfully as to foster a sixteen-year binge of financial speculation in everything from common stocks to Beanie Babies. It is from such antecedents that severe deflations have always developed.

Moreover, this boom has been the longest sustained period of rapidly rising investment prices in the history of the country. It has brought about the greatest increase in stock prices over such a period in the history of finance going back at least 300 years. The magnitude of the coming deflation is likely to be commensurate.

Deflations that follow such episodes are not "good." They do not "pad profits." They always lead to depression. The reason they do so is that at the peak, so many people have a stake in continuously rising asset prices that the dramatic reversal of their fortunes forces them to slash spending, which induces economic contraction.

Like inflation, deflation is a process, not an event. It has been sneaking up to the U.S. slowly. Japan has been leading the way, its deflation having begun in 1990. Six years later, the dollar prices of gold, precious metals stocks, oil and the commodity indexes started down in earnest, signaling a spread in the deflationary attitude to the rest of the world. In 1997-1998, deflation struck the Pacific Rim, as its currencies, debt paper and stocks collapsed, dragging economies with them. In April 1998, the average stock in the U.S. (as measured by the advance-decline line and the Value Line Composite geometric index) may have started to fall. In July, high-yield bonds slipped. In September and October, emerging-market debt prices crashed. The U.S. gross domestic product, which lags market trends, has been slowing for months. These are classic precursors to a larger contraction in investment markets, retail prices and the economy.

The signal that the trend toward deflation is accelerating will come with a crash in stock prices and a reversal of the real estate boom. When the amount of outstanding debt/credit begins to contract and the savings rate reverses its persistent downtrend, deflationary psychology will be entrenched.

There is far less to fear about deflation than there is to fear about the denial of its nature and consequences. Any informed person can prepare financially for a serious deflation and be positioned to take immense advantage of the investment bargains that become available at its end. The truly unfortunate people will be those who suffer financial destruction because they were told that deflation is implausible or that it is benign, good for the economy and nothing to fear. To the contrary, it will devastate those who make either assumption. It can benefit only those who do not.

— Robert R. Prechter, Jr.
President, Elliott Wave International

The Elliott Wave Theorist
Special Report

September 17, 1998

The Decoupling Arrives

by EWI bond analyst David Lockwood

Today (September 17, 1998), *The New York Times* expressed shock at the "decoupling of fixed income," i.e., the worldwide collapse in low-grade debt concurrent with soaring prices for high-grade debt. It also said that the debacle and decoupling were unpredictable:

> Doesn't Investing 101 dictate that when interest rates fall, bond prices rise? Indeed it does. But Investing 101 *could not have predicted* the confluence of events – the work of professional investors, hedge fund managers and brokerage trading desks, who *ran away from anything with a whiff of risk to it* – that have *paralyzed worldwide bond markets*. As the herd stampeded out of junk bonds, convertible debt, emerging market bonds, even relatively unrisky corporate issues, *buyers for these securities disappeared.*

It is true that "Investing 101" could not have predicted this stunning contrasting picture. Could anyone have predicted it?

At the Crest of the Tidal Wave was published three years ago. Its purpose was to prepare you for the second major financial change of the past two decades. Read our description of coming events and see if it sounds like what is happening today:

> It is a confusing paradox that a depression produces trends toward both higher *and* lower interest rates, the trend determinant being *perceived default risk*. While interest rates rise on weak debt, they fall on guaranteed strong debt (except for a brief time when the crisis temporarily forces strapped investors to raise cash).... As the chances of a borrower's survival is perceived to worsen, credit-providing investors demand higher rates in an attempt to get back as much of their investment as possible. ...High and rising interest rates in evidence for many issues reflect not inflation or a desire to borrow, but people's increasing fear of losing their principal.
> ...As interest rates paid by issuers of questionable reliability soar, those

paid by borrowers of perceived impeccable reliability fall to extremely low levels as investors search not for income but for a safe haven. This movement is classically termed a "flight to quality." Any debt that is perceived to be risky falls in price along with the contraction in the economy, and the greater the contraction, the further the fall. ...So while today every bondholder is convinced that a poor economy means rising prices, history will reveal that on a larger scale, a poor economy means default.

Emerging Market Debt

At the Crest added that the meltdown in high-yield rates would un-questionably extend to the so-called "emerging markets":

What is the future for "emerging country" debt? It is no coinci-dence that recent years have witnessed the first craze for Latin American debt since (guess when) the *late 1920s*. Shortly after that time, almost every South American government defaulted. Such defaults are sure to occur again soon, and on a far bigger scale.

Over and over, we were told that our analysis was too radical, that the U.S. Treasury, the World Bank and the IMF would never let "emerging market" bonds collapse. *The New York Times* has just addressed the new reality on that front as well:

As long as the International Monetary Fund was willing to bail out countries experiencing economic disarray, investors were comfortable investing in fledgling markets. Russia changed all that. Now investors want to go all the way to the ultimate quality of U.S. Treasury securities. Nothing in between seems safe enough.

We did not *guess* that the IMF would prove a useless tool against contractionary psychology. We *knew* it. When panic strikes, the underly-ing emotional nature of markets is most evident. Only Russia has so far suffered an outright economic meltdown, yet all of the charts look nearly identical. We said that emerging markets would soon become "submerging markets." The charts on the next page graphically display the amazing event that our monetary analysis back in 1995 predicted as inevitable.

U.S. Junk Bonds and REITS

The concern we expressed in *At the Crest* extended to low-grade U.S. debt issues. We dedicated an entire chapter to U.S. high-yield "junk" bonds

HIGH-GRADE AND LOW-GRADE BONDS DECOUPLE

<table>
<tr><td align="center">Low-Grade
"Emerging Market" Debt</td><td align="center">Currently High-Grade
Government Debt</td></tr>
</table>

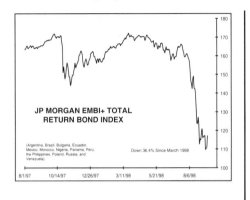

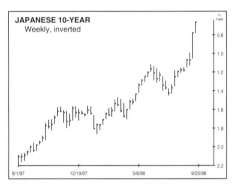

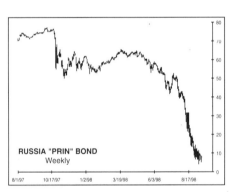

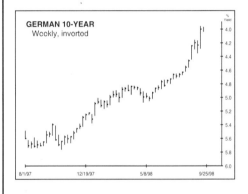

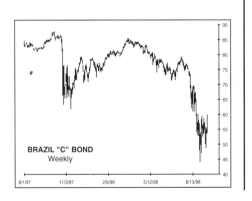

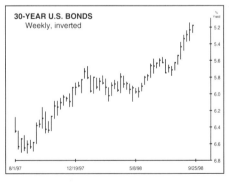

Figure 1

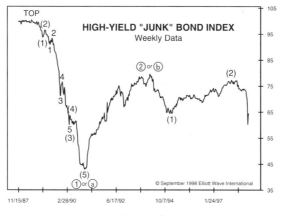

Figure 2

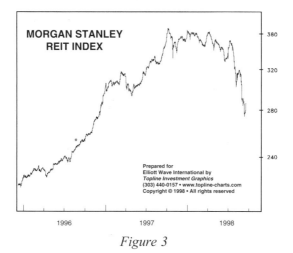

Figure 3

and another section to real estate investment trusts (REITs) that represent portfolios of mortgage debt and presented this conclusion:

Investors are focusing only on the promised rate of interest and not on the safety of their principal. Because only *yield*, not *quality*, is an issue among investors, the desire to invest in junk bonds has been of historic proportion. Such manias are always followed by disappointment. Wave 3 down, which is now in its early stages of development, will be *more* destructive to values than wave 1. First waves are surprises, but third waves feed on bad news. The only thing holding up this index is the entrenched belief that the economy is safe. This delusion will dissolve quickly when the economic statistics begin coming in below expectations.

Then owners of junk bonds will become concerned not with the return *on* their principal, but with the return *of* it. The depression will reveal why they call them junk. If the depression is even half as deep as the waves suggest, it will force the issuers to default.

Was this language too strong? Just ask the investors who did not heed the warning in *At the Crest of the Tidal Wave* and kept buying junk and REITS month after month when they were yielding just 2.75 points above Treasuries.

The Extent of the Losses

Here is a good summary of what investors have suffered, from *The New York Times*:

> Toting up the dollars lost by investors in bonds in August is diffi-cult because of the market's opaqueness: $48 billion was lost in emerging market debt that was denominated in dollars, $14.6 billion disappeared from portfolios of convertible bonds, another $15 billion was likely lost in junk bonds and $1.67 billion disappeared during the month from an index of real estate investment trusts that invest in mortgage securities. That's about $80 billion lost.

These losses hit hedge fund managers hardest. Many of them "hedged" big bets on emerging markets by selling U.S. Treasuries short. In other words, these managers bet against *both* cases presented in *At the Crest* and were heavily invested on the wrong side of *both markets*. The results have been a disaster. Unfortunately, big players have not been the only victims. Read what is happening to "average investors":

> Investors who are not yet aware of the recent turmoil in bonds may get an unpleasant jolt when they check their mutual fund holdings. There are plenty of bondholders out there: as of Sept. 9, according to AMG Data Services, assets held in bond funds totaled $533 billion, roughly one-fifth the amount currently held in stock funds.

The junk bond chart may not look *that* bad yet, but the actual damage to date is much worse than it shows. *The Elliott Wave Theorist* has often cautioned that playing the low-quality investment game, whether in bonds or stocks, is fraught with risk because when the trend changes, *there are no buyers*. Read this, again from the *The New York Times*:

Investors who think that September's relative calm in the market is a sign of stability should not be confused. It is a frozen market, where nobody's selling because there are no buyers. Dealers at major Wall Street brokerage firms are no longer bidding for bonds from their customers; they will only take an order if they know they have another customer interested in owning the bonds. And since few investors are interested in adding to their bond positions until they see the market stabilize, most sell orders don't get executed.

As a result, the losses that have been registered in the charts of low-grade bonds so far probably reflect only a fraction of the real damage done to these markets. If there were more actual selling going on, the prices would be far lower. At this point, there is no prospect of recovery in these issues.

The Only Source of News in Advance

Six months after publication of *At the Crest*, the worldwide deflation that we predicted began, as commodities, precious metals and mining stocks started down. We at Elliott Wave International did everything we could to protect people. Spending more on advertising than we made on the book, we sold 27,000 copies of *At the Crest* before the final high in U.S. stocks [per the Value Line index and the a/d line] and the last day of liquidity for low-grade bonds.

Many more of the predicted financial, monetary and economic events lie ahead of us than behind us, so *At the Crest* remains the most current book on markets that you can read today. As you can see by the predictions that are coming true month after month, it is more current than tomorrow's newspaper.

Staying Safe

The New York Times, echoing the sentiment of virtually everyone, says, "Treasuries are as close to a risk-free investment as there is." If you think that the "high-grade" debt issues shown in Figure 1 are permanently safe havens for your capital, re-read Chapter 16 of *At the Crest of the Tidal Wave*. Far more dramatic headlines lie ahead than we have seen to date.

Elliott Wave Investing

by EWI foreign stock analyst, William Mitchell

While many factors such as language, culture and economy differentiate nations around the world, each shares one common ingredient in its financial markets: crowd psychology. The driving force behind whether an index goes up or down is people's expectations about the market's future direction. The prevailing sentiment does not necessarily involve every individual, but in aggregate, the people participating in the markets are acting as a crowd.

From a practical standpoint, the goal of any analytical method is to identify market lows suitable for buying and market highs suitable for selling. The Wave Principle is a useful tool for this endeavor. Ralph Nelson Elliott discovered that crowd behavior, as expressed in stock prices, trends and reverses in recognizable patterns. Every market goes through a set of stages to get from bottom to top and back again. Each major market advance begins from a point of extreme pessimism at a low and carries to a point of excessive optimism at a top. Along the way, the same stages of psychology develop on the short term, medium term and long term as part of the progression. To be successful on an international scale, one must be able to determine where an individual market is within its overall trend.

Just as capital appreciation is the objective in a bull market, capital preservation is equally important in a bear market. To achieve this end, one needs to recognize when to be invested and when it is time to step aside. This is one of the primary differences between a market-timing and a stock-selecting system. An investor using the Wave Principle looks for the best opportunities among markets. He is not always invested, so he risks missing out on some market moves. On the other hand, the typical fund manager is nearly always invested. In most years, this is a successful strategy as the market is generally in an advancing trend. When the trend changes, however, virtually all issues are swept lower, regardless of their relative valuation. According to Lipper Analytical Services, only 8 of 3300 U.S. stock funds gained in value in August.

Bear markets are quite capable of retracting a considerable portion of the previous advance in a short amount of time. Just ask a Southeast Asian investor. While a brilliant stock selector may outperform the benchmark index on a relative basis during a bear market, this achievement means simply that one will lose, for example, only 41% instead of 45%. In actual fact, most stock selectors do worse than the averages in a bear market because the broad list of stocks tends to underperform blue chips in a serious decline. At Elliott Wave International, we do our best to avoid these debacles.

For example, in just 18 months, Malaysian stocks have retraced over 10 years' worth of stock market gains. In April of 1997, the Wave Principle indicated that Malaysian stocks were completing a five-wave pattern from the 1970s (see Figure 1). The pattern implied that we should see the largest decline in over 20 years. This devastating drop occurred, and it has certainly changed the crowd's opinion about the market.

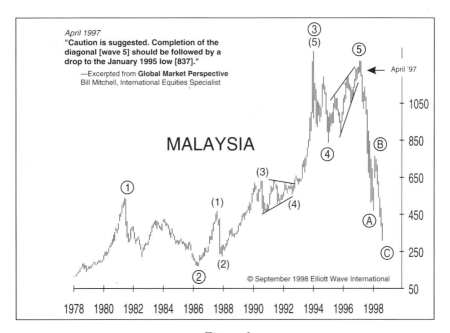

Figure 1

Just over a year ago, Hong Kong reverted to Chinese rule amid much fanfare, and crowd expectations were tremendously optimistic. Investors stormed the bourse, and volume on the exchange quickly swelled to unheard-of levels. However, the Wave Principle signaled that it was time to avoid Hong Kong stocks (see Figure 2). We recognized a completed pattern paired with an extreme in sentiment. This combination indicated a significant retrenchment in prices. In the span of 12 months, Hong Kong stocks have dissolved five years' worth of gains.

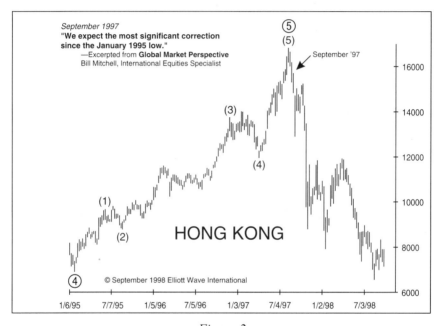

Figure 2

As stretched as many Asian markets were on the upside, they have now fallen to low valuations. The overall social mood has turned 180 degrees, creating the psychological backdrop for a bottom. We are simply waiting for a full bear market pattern to resolve so we can turn bullish.

It is crucial to know the difference between the start of a bear market and simply a correction within an ongoing trend. While the markets in Hong Kong and Malaysia displayed completed long-term structures in 1997, German equities did not. As a result, we were able to recognize the October 1997 sell-off in German stocks as a correction within an ongoing uptrend

Figure 3

(see Figure 3). This perspective enabled us to stay bullish on Germany and most other European markets through the first half of this year while avoiding most Asian markets' major bear trends.

The Wave Principle signals in advance the relative magnitude of the next period of progress or regress in markets. Our job is to read those signals, and while we do stumble occasionally, most of the time, we provide a very useful perspective.

December 4, 1998

A Peek at the Future

In the U.S., the slow roll of this long-term peak has frustrated many a bear, us included, as we have watched our deflationary outlook unfold throughout much of the rest of the world. The emotional drain of the latest high in the Dow has caused a handful of our domestic subscribers to pack it in (for their reasoning, visit Bob's Billboard at elliottwave.com). It is interesting to compare their frustration to the near total affirmation we receive from many foreign subscribers. As D.C. in Mildura, Australia puts it: "From the financial press here in Australia over the past few months, one could be excused for thinking they were publishing excerpts from your book rather than reporting actual economic events from around the world." In Hong Kong, where the decline is deeper, the feedback we receive reflects an even stronger sense of conviction that *At the Crest*'s vision is correct. Here is a letter we received from the heart of the bear market:

> November 17, 1998
> If I read *At the Crest* last year, I would be much better off, and my parents wouldn't have lost so much money. I returned to Hong Kong from [California in June 1997], to witness the historical handover of Hong Kong back to China and to start a new university job. The first thing my mother told me to do was to buy an apartment because in her own words, "If prices keep on increasing, you will never be able to afford one." Being a physician, if I cannot afford one, how many other citizens would be able to? Prices more or less quadrupled as everyone went into a speculative frenzy. Even taxi drivers and little old ladies in the market were talking about the stock market and the real estate market. I concluded that it was crazy to buy at that point. The stock market was something else; anything to do with Mainland China would appreciate no matter what. A penny stock called CNPC, which explores oil on the mainland, went from an IPO of 10 cents to $5 within a matter of months. Then, there were the "Red Chips," companies that do business in China. You could pretty much put China onto anything and it would turn into gold.

My friends installed terminals in their clinics and stopped seeing pa-
tients. Many of them were boasting how much money they were making,
certainly much more than most doctors. A friend of mine put all his savings into the stock market and borrowed up to the limit of margin
requirements. Even my wife bought a couple of Chinese "H-shares" based
on tips from my mother-in-law! (Investment for my wife usually means
T-bills.) Then, on October 28, everything came apart. First, the index fell
from 16,600 to 12,000. It maintained that level long enough to lure back
in the optimists. Then, it went down to 8000. Everybody started blaming
the hedge funds and George Soros in particular. The government was the
most vocal. Then, the index plunged to 6600. The government decided
to intervene and bought up 15% of the Hang Seng index constituents.
With the recent Fed rate cut, the Hang Seng is back to around 10,000, but
for how long? To those skeptics who sneer at the predictions in *At The
Crest*, I only have this to say; you have to live through it to believe it, but
it really can happen, even if it seems impossible at the moment, just as it
was in Hong Kong in June 1997.

—Dr. Wu, Hong Kong

We think people were right in 1997 when they said, "Asia is the future." The gory details now include a 7% quarterly GDP decline in Hong
Kong, the island's biggest quarterly decline ever. The figure dwarfs the
previous record of 4.7% set in the third quarter of 1974. Over the past year,
property values have declined 40%. In China, the government clings to
contentions of 4% unemployment and 8% growth, but observers say growth
has actually slowed to non-existent and unemployment is probably higher
than unofficial World Bank estimates of 8%. Competition is so fierce as
deflation takes hold that Beijing is now setting *minimum* prices for products and services in 21 different industries. Despite the measures, prices
fell almost 3% in October alone. Angry investors have staged the "boldest
protest in the Chinese capital since the 1989 Tiananmen Square demonstra-
tions." Gitic corporation, the shining financial star behind the office towers,
five-star hotels and six-lane highways of Gangzhou and one of the highest
fliers of 1997, has been shut down.

A broader look at Asia offers an even more gruesome portrait. Car
sales are off 70% in Thailand. Jakarta office rental rates fell by half from
April to June 1998. Japan's bad public-sector debt amounts to 20-25% of
GDP. Bad private-sector debt pushes the total figure to as much as 60%.
The only industry that is growing is the "alibi" business, in which agencies

create fake lives for the unemployed. "We often take on the role of pretend employer," explains a man who runs an agency in Tokyo's nightlife district. We could go on and on, but you get the idea. Don't look now, but despite all the carnage, "There is a new optimism rising in Asia." Brokerage firms, economists and *The New York Times* have signaled that "the crisis has bottomed out." The near-unanimity on this point in the U.S. is a *guarantee* that the news is going to get still worse. As it rolls in, Americans have a huge advantage over their Asian counterparts. They can see the headlines months and months ahead of time. Most, however, will have to "live through it to believe it."

Esquire Magazine
(excerpt)

February 1999

Game Over

by Ken Kurson

It's a beautiful piece of writing:

"He looked away from the buildings and out over the ocean of trees. Since Atlanta was not a port city and was, in fact, far inland, the trees stretched on in every direction. They were Atlanta's greatest natural resource, those trees were. People loved to live beneath them." That's Tom Wolfe in *A Man in Full,* but his anxious magnate Charlie Croker isn't the only one looking up wistfully at those Atlanta trees. Every day, Robert Prechter glances skyward and is amazed that the sky hasn't fallen.

Prechter is the popularizer of the Elliott wave theory, which suggests that commerce, and life in general, follows a five-wave pattern with peaks and valleys that can be predicted. He became marvelously, ridiculously famous in the early eighties for correctly predicting that U.S. equities were about to enter a bull market; his face was constantly on television, he had a best-seller, and his predictions were widely heeded. Nowadays, it's hard to imagine our darling stock market being shunned by investors. But those who recall gas lines, 15 percent inflation, and $850 ounces of gold know that believers in the stock market then were as crackpot and rare as those today who expect the market to crash back down to the triple digits. Prechter's 1982 call was made against a backdrop of overwhelming skepticism. It's sweet to be right. It's sweeter to be right when disagreeing with everyone else. But if there's one thing the public loves more than elevating a guru when he's right, it's kicking the crap out of him when he's wrong.

After calling for a bull market at around Dow 800, Prechter stayed bullish pretty much through the eighties. When the crash of 1987 obliterated many investors, Prechter got thrown out with the bathwater. Ironically, Prechter was one of the very few to be 100 percent *out* of equities on Black Monday, October 19, having gotten out at the very top of the sucker's rally on October 5. But because of his identification with the bull run (and because his revised forecast called for a higher top than the 2,700 after which the market cratered), Prechter's goose was cooked. The vitriol his critics brought to the ritual flaying was shocking, especially since most of it came from the same people who'd elevated him to such a lofty pedestal.

"Any human being finds reversals of fortune difficult," Prechter concedes with characteristic detachment before launching into an even more characteristic explanation for the change in the public's perception of him. "I had a huge psychological advantage because I knew exactly what was happening. A rising public persona *is* a bull market. I plotted my subscription numbers and saw five waves up, ending in late 1987. I stopped making media forecasts in September. The worst thing is to be on the firing line when the sharpshooters start blasting. The attacks on my persona began in 1988, even though 1988 was one of my best forecasting years, when I was ranked in the top two in stocks and bonds." See, the beauty of Prechter's system is that *everything* — stock markets, hemlines, the dopiness of song lyrics — oscillates in predictable five-wave patterns. To Prechter, microscopic dividend yields and the rise of Hanson are equally reliable indicators of financial troubles ahead.

Prechter has avoided the media for the most part since '87, but he's hardly disappeared. His Atlanta operation boasts seventy employees, his chat boards are smart and active, and his newsletters and books still sell well. While his critics claim that his constant bear-market forecasts these days are like a broken clock that's inevitably right, but only twice a day, in fact he's had a pretty decent run lately, calling the July top and predicting that the broader indexes would not match the heights of the Dow. Though he'll never again command the kind of attention that used to come so easily, Prechter insists he doesn't miss his old spot in the oracle's seat. "I appreciate and value my supporters far more than I am annoyed by critics," he says. Prechter's also sticking to his guns as he waits for the delirium of America's investors to fade into panic. Answering the it's-different-this-time folks, Prechter points to the great bear markets of the past. "You get 'new paradigm' talk at every major market peak. They were saying the same kinds of things in 1929 and 1720. It is a psychological phenomenon. The main goal of market discourse is the rationalization of unconscious, impulsive judgments. When future generations look back at this peak, they will say it was obvious in figures such as the dividend yield. Practically speaking, why should anyone want to own a piece of a company that pays them nothing? The only answer is, because someone else will pay more.

But why should anyone pay more if he, too, gets nothing? All he gets is the opportunity to sell it to someone else who presumably will pay yet more for nothing. This is tulip mania."

An embarrassing public defeat has left Prechter defensive but unbowed, shaken but not stirred. But then, all he lost was a bit of reputation and a lot of status. But the markets go on — and they forgive you, if you let them.

© 1999 *Esquire* magazine
reprinted with permission

[*Note: A word to the wise: Markets never forgive people when they're wrong, me included. —Ed.*]

Bridge News

July 6, 1999

Technical Analysis Profile:
Robert Prechter

by Kira McCaffrey Brecht, reporter

As an undergraduate at Yale University, Robert Prechter started keeping a chart of the gold market and watching it from a rudimentary Elliott wave basis. The Elliott bug bit him as his wave forecasts hit their targets in the early years of the massive bull market that ultimately drove gold above $800 in early 1980. He has come under fire in recent years because of his unwavering calls for a stock market top, but still expects to see a major retracement, even calling for the Dow to slide below 1000 at some point.

Bob Prechter, who played a big role in putting Elliott wave analysis on the map in the 1980s, has taken the Elliott wave principles and formed them into a fascinating mix of social and financial theories. Currently president of Elliott Wave International in Gainesville, Ga., he has built his career on the Wave Principle, expanding the theory to include human social behavior as it manifests itself in the economy and financial markets.

Elliott wave analysis, developed by Ralph Elliott, is based on repetitive wave patterns, which in turn reflect the Fibonacci number sequence. Very simplistically, an ideal Elliott pattern is a 5-wave advance followed by a 3-wave decline.

Herd Instincts

"At Yale, I kept signing up for mass psychology courses," Prechter says. "I never made the connection between that and speculative finance until years later when I realized that they are the same field."

Pointing to research on the limbic system, the more primitive area of the brain that relates to survival and fear, Prechter observes that these "impulsive, not rational, actions help organisms survive in primitive circumstances.

"Organisms flock or herd together in a group. If you are in a group, your odds are better for survival. If one animal is running, others tend to follow even if they don't know why that first animal is running. It's not rational thinking, but it's not completely random, either. Unfortunately, such impulsive behavior does not enhance survival in all modern circumstances."

Drawing an analogy to stock investors, he says, "This thinking is impulsive and patterned. The tape is nothing but the herd. As investors see prices race up and down, they jump in and out. That is the origin of waves—the patterns in which humans herd.

"The stock market is a direct recording of social mood. It moves up and down as people change their collective thinking. The social mood has been expansive for the past decade and has resulted in an expansive economy.

"During a mood expansion, people buy stocks, expand their businesses and take more risks. Optimism and ebullience cause like behaviors in all other fields as well, which is why social and financial trends correlate."

Lengthy "Mania" in Stocks

As the U.S. equity market has charged higher in recent years, etching the greatest bull market in history on the charts, Prechter admits, "I've been premature in thinking that we are late in the cycle. But it's unprecedented to have a manic mood expand for 17 years."

He examined 300 years of financial history and concludes that the current "mania" is the longest. He says the "tulip bulb" and "South Sea" bubbles, in Holland and Europe in the 1630s and about 1718, respectively, lasted only 2 to 3 years. The "mania" in the U.S. markets in the 1920s lasted 8 years, and a similar type of bubble occurred in Japan from 1974 to 1989, leaving the current U.S. experience — which Prechter defines as having begun in 1982 — as the longest.

"We are at extremes that have never been recorded in history," he says. He points to the low dividend payout — currently between zero and 1.5% for the major averages — and evaporating book values as examples.

"It's certainly never been that low in the U.S. before," he says. "If people are not receiving a dividend and own little underlying property, that means the only reason they are holding that stock is because they believe it will go up in price."

Using history as a potential gauge for future activity, Prechter says, "Every mania has been followed by a crash in values that brought prices below their starting point."

Pointing to the crash in European stock markets after the South Sea bubble, he observes that the average stock price plummeted by 98%. The 1920s bull market was followed by a slide of 89%. The Nikkei sank 65% to its 1998 low, and "it's not over yet."

Technical Situation Deteriorating

Looking at the current bull market, Prechter says he thinks that in the major advance from the Depression low of 1932, the fifth wave of activity began in 1982. Once that fifth wave completes, "the entire bull market of the 1980s and 1990s will be retraced," he says. "The Dow will be back in triple digits before it's over.

"Some people say I'm forecasting the end of the world, but that's not true. The 1929-1932 drop was the most severe in our experience, and we had the Depression, but it was not the end of the world."

Examining the market from a traditional perspective, he says, "The technical situation is deteriorating. The rate of upside change is slowing. Optimism among traders, advisors and consumers is on the ceiling. There are many, many signs that we are very, very late in the cycle."

Prechter declined to offer a specific forecast in terms of timing. "I've already shown that I don't know the month or even the year of the top," he said. "What I'm quite sure of is that the major move is so mature and extended that the intelligent thing to do is prepare for a reversal. By the time a bear market in blue-chips is clearly visible, many stocks typically are already down 50%."

To prepare for this downturn, Prechter suggests, "Convert to cash. The safest things to be in are cash equivalents, which include T-bills."

Looking at Social Behavior

In recent years, Prechter has incorporated social behavior into his market analysis.

"The Wave Principle describes a form of collective human herding behavior," he says. "Behavior governs social mood, which results in social action and creates social history."

From a social standpoint, he says, there is a lot of evidence that the current bull market cycle is mature.

Examples of the optimistic and ebullient social mood currently include "essentially worldwide peace," he says. "Wars tend to follow bear markets as they are a result of a negative, fearful and angry social mood."

He cited the Revolutionary War, the Civil War and World War II as examples of wars that followed major bear markets.

"The fact that you can look around the world and see very little fighting and people getting along quite well is a reflection of the fact that the social mood trend has been up for a long time," he says.

During the past several hundred years, Prechter says, "Technology crazes have come near the end of major cycles. In the early 1830s, it was a flood of inventions such as the camera and the telegraph. In the 1920s, it was radio, air travel and so on. In the 1990s, it's the Internet."

Popularity of Certain Sports

Another social observation from Prechter is that certain sports are popular during bull markets — particularly basketball and baseball. He sees the recent professional sporting craze as yet another sign that the cycle high is nearing.

"You see tremendous dominance by a particular popular team, team expansions, major stars and the breaking of old statistics—like the home run record," he said. "This is a result of certain talented people feeding off of the rise of social mood and providing nearly superhuman performance. That these sports today are providing breakthrough statistics supports the idea of an extreme as well," he says.

In bear markets, these same aspects of the sport dwindle.

Looking at the sports analogy from a different angle, Prechter says that baseball attendance records per team peaked out in 1993, along with the stock prices of card manufacturers such as Topps. These events in themselves could be a sort of technical bearish divergence within the social mood, suggesting that a change is in the wind.

"The lyrics in pop music are pretty ebullient these days in a different way from the '70s," he adds.

Overall, Prechter says, "these trends are coincident. It is not that one precedes another; they are all a direct reflection of the same mood."

Expectations of Deflation

Shifting gears over to the commodity markets, Prechter does not expect to see any major bottoms in price near term.

"We experienced increasing inflation into early 1980," he explains. "From that year forward, we have enjoyed disinflation and the stock mania. In Asia, the markets collapsed and they are deflating. As for the U.S.,

I'm anticipating the onset of deflation and the end of two decades of disinflation."

He points to gold's recent push to 20-year lows and the breakdown of the Bridge/CRB index as "early warning" signs of the impending deflationary environment.

When asked whether he sees global money flowing into Japan from the U.S., his answer is no: "A lot of people have a misconception that if money goes out of one market, it has to go into another. In a deflationary environment, almost all assets go down in price. Historically, we've tended to see all areas of the western world deflate at the same time. The 'money' — actually credit — just disappears."

Looking at current conditions worldwide, he thinks that "the decade-long deflationary environment in Japan was an early falling domino."

Despite his expectations of deflation, he doesn't necessarily see the bond market as a safe haven for cash.

"Most people say that if you expect deflation, you should buy bonds," Prechter said. "This is true if you can buy bonds that will remain AAA.

"In the 1930s, U.S. government bonds underwent a short shake-out, but they basically held their value. They were issued by a strong government and in a very small quantity compared to today."

He points to interest rates at 15% in the late 1970s and says, "The overall rate of inflation is slowing. When it crosses zero, we will have deflation."

Returning to gold, the first market Prechter began charting with the Elliott principle, he says, "for a couple of decades, I've had a long-term downside target in gold, and I think we will get there."

Although he declined to specifically identify his target, he offered that it was "below $200 per ounce," adding, "as soon as we reach the depth of the deflationary move, I think gold and silver will be the bargains of a lifetime."

Some Markets Do Better with Elliott Analysis

Looking at the nuts and bolts of Elliott analysis, Prechter thinks this method is advantageous because "the wave structure of the stock market subsumes all technical indicators. The indicators tell you about the status of the market, but ultimately they are products of the market. Market action, however, is a product of the Wave Principle."

He points to overbought/oversold indicators and says that the stock market was "overbought years ago" but prices kept going up. Some critics of Elliott analysis fault the theory's potential for subjectivity in counting the waves. Prechter counters by saying, "It is an objective discipline, but it only speaks to probabilities.... It says, 'this is more likely than that.'

"Even so, sometimes the critics are right because a particular practitioner is not prioritizing his probabilities correctly. Every human, including me, is under influences we have to struggle to overcome."

Prechter admits that there are certain markets in which Elliott analysis tends to work better than others. He points to the stock and gold markets as two particularly suited to wave analysis.

"These markets reflect social mood in general, which tends to reflect the Wave Principle," he says. "The worst are the meats."

He says the livestock market's interdependence on some of the agricultural markets for feed could complicate those markets' influences.

Also, "some of the small currencies don't seem to follow the Wave Principle very well," he says. "Because they are minor markets, mass psychology has less freedom to express itself with abandon."

Looking at the commodity markets, Prechter thinks that during inflationary times, one can see waves develop clearly, while during periods of "monetary calm," the markets tended to "meander."

He concludes, "Waves are not simply an artifact of the stock market; they are the pulse of our society."

July 19, 1999

You Heard It Here First

Many of you will recall having read a Special Report to *The Elliott Wave Theorist* titled "Bulls, Bears and Manias," which was published on May 21, 1997. That report contained the following paragraph:

"In all these cases, the client becomes livid. 'How can my market timer not see that stocks always go up?! How can this stodgy value buyer sit year after year in stocks that are stuck in the mud?! Why does my advisor have my account 40% in bonds and 10% in bills when obviously the action is in the stock market?! What's wrong with my broker? Almost everything he picks goes down! How come my fund is lagging the S&P by so much? What am I paying those guys for?! ***Everybody's getting rich but me!***'"

It took two years, but finally a popular national magazine has caught up with our observation and nearly our exact phrasing as well.

December 1999

An Overview of the Long Term Elliott Wave Case for Stocks

Evidence at Supercycle Degree

By "Supercycle" degree, we mean the size of wave that has taken the Dow Jones Industrial Average up from its low at 41.22 in July 1932 up to the present. Figure 1 shows the standard depiction of an Elliott wave. Has the Supercycle advance followed this picture?

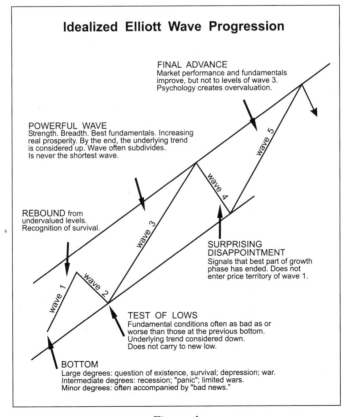

Figure 1

Figure 2 shows that we can certainly label the Supercycle advance as a five-wave structure. However, can we be sure that what we label wave V from 1974 is not something else, say, part of a third-wave extension?

Figure 2

Pay particular attention to the descriptions attending "wave 3" and "wave 5" in Figure 1. They explain that wave 5 is always weaker than wave 3 in both "technical" and "fundamental" terms. Specifically, this description means that advancing fifth waves are *narrower* in terms of the number of stocks participating on the upside and have *weaker* economic consequences.

Figure 3 displays the advance-decline line, which reflects the net percentage of stocks rising vs. falling day after day on the New York Stock Exchange. Note that the rise of 1942-1966 was significantly broader than

Figure 3

Figure 4

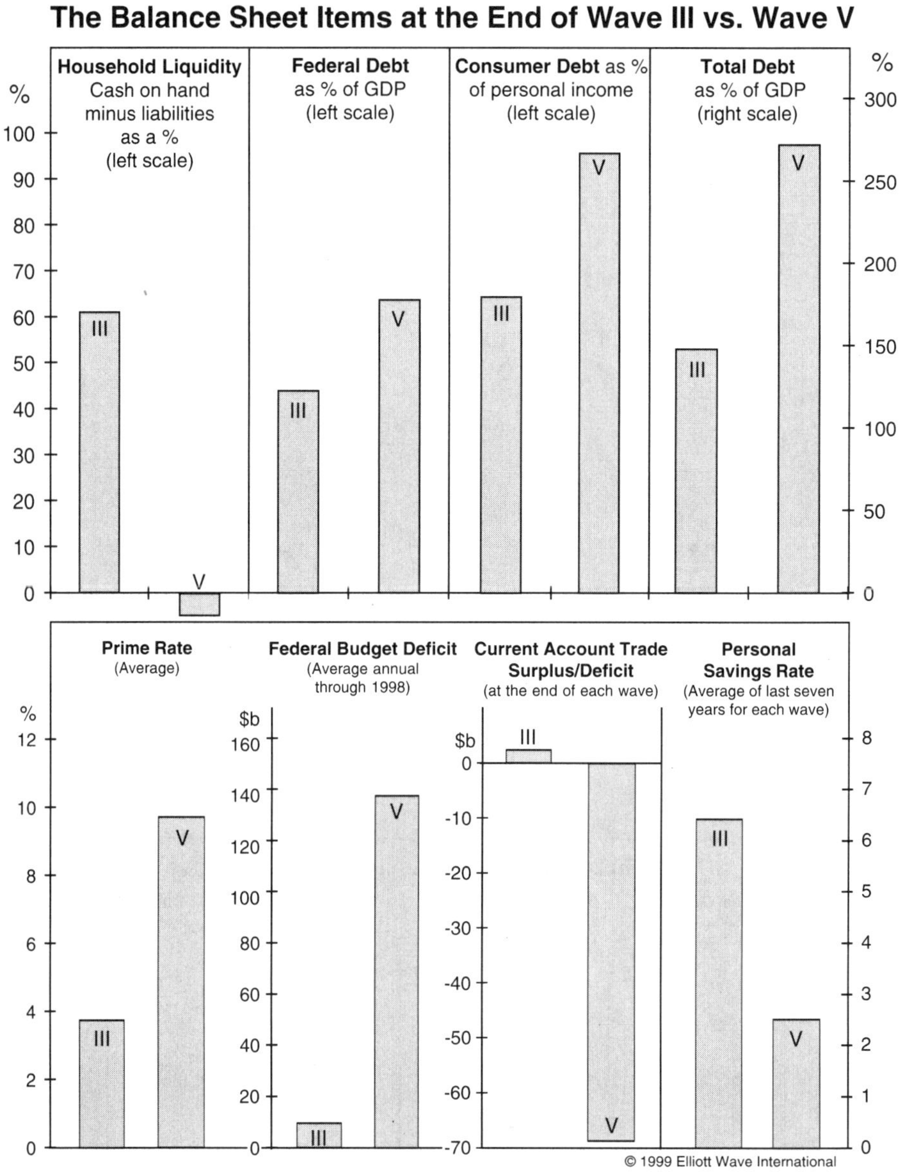
The Balance Sheet Items at the End of Wave III vs. Wave V
Household Liquidity
Cash on hand minus liabilities as a % (left scale)
Federal Debt
as % of GDP (left scale)
Consumer Debt as % of personal income (left scale)
Total Debt
as % of GDP (right scale)
%
100
90
80
70
60
50
40
30
20
10
0
300
250
200
150
100
50
III
V
Prime Rate
(Average)
Federal Budget Deficit
(Average annual through 1998)
Current Account Trade Surplus/Deficit
(at the end of each wave)
Personal Savings Rate
(Average of last seven years for each wave)
$b
12
10
8
6
4
2
160
140
120
100
80
60
40
20
-10
-20
-30
-40
-50
-60
-70
7
5
3
1
© 1999 Elliott Wave International

Figure 5

the one beginning in 1974. This means that in *technical* terms, the latter period has been narrower, fitting the classic behavior of a fifth wave.

Figure 4 displays statistics showing the difference between the economic performance resulting from the 1942-1966 advance and that resulting from the advance since 1974. Figure 5 displays statistics on the difference between the monetary and financial underpinnings of the two periods. In every category, the latter period is revealed to have been weaker. These comparative "fundamentals" fit the classic environment of a fifth wave.

Figures 3 through 5 show that our labeling of the Supercycle's subdivisions is correct, beyond doubt. The advance from 1974 is a fifth wave.

Evidence at Cycle Degree

By "Cycle" degree, we mean the size of wave that has taken the Dow Jones Industrial Average up from its low at 577.60 in December 1974 up to the present. This wave, like so many Elliott waves, has taken a classic shape. Figure 6 shows a diverse selection of long-term advances that unfolded between parallel lines. As you look over these examples, reflect upon the diverse, typically wild, social settings during which each occurred. Despite all events, the tendency of the Wave Principle to effect movements within trend channels was satisfied as if there were no attending events at all.

SAMPLE ELLIOTT WAVES

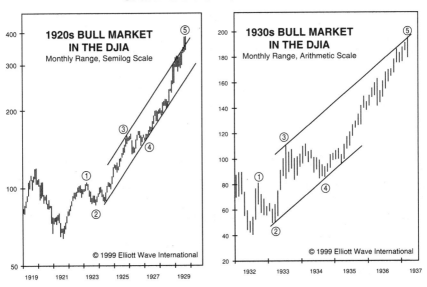

Figure 6a

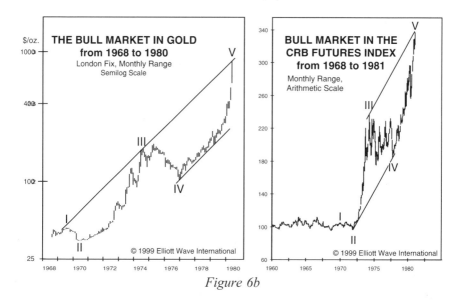

Figure 6b

Wave V has performed the same feat as these other markets. The trend channel for Cycle wave V shown in Figure 7 is constructed according to Elliott's primary approach, which is to connect the lows of waves two and four and then draw a parallel line touching the top of wave three.

The action during 1997-1999, moreover, has been quite similar to that of 1928-1929. Prices have clustered near the upper trendline, breaking through it briefly in what Elliott called a "throw-over." As noted often in these pages, a throw-over is more likely when a market slips below the lower trendline early in the wave's development, as this one did in 1982.

Figure 8 shows an alternative trend channel that allows a bit more room on the upside. It is less orthodox than the one show in Figure 7 but neatly contains all the price action.

Evidence at Grand Supercycle Degree

By "Grand Supercycle" degree, we mean the size of wave that has taken stock prices up from their low in 1784 up to the present. Figure 9 shows our depiction of the Grand Supercycle advance. Once again, the question is whether this wave may be better labeled as a developing extension, suggesting decades or centuries more advance before the Grand Supercycle peaks.

Figure 7

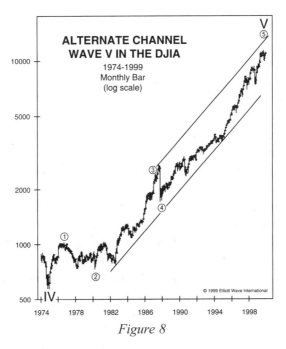

Figure 8

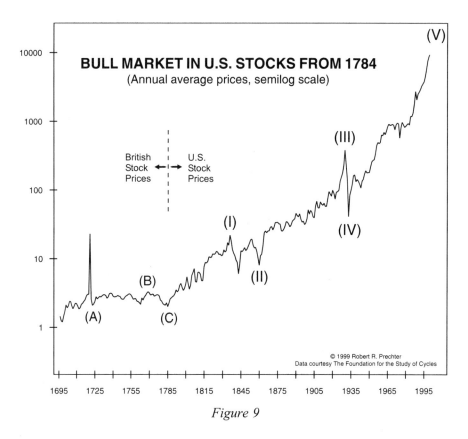

Figure 9

While comparative statistics are hard to come by, Figure 10 shows one measure that supports our case for a top of no less than Grand Supercycle degree in the making. Here, stock valuation is expressed in terms of annualized dividend yield so that the lower the dividend payout, the higher stocks are priced, and vice versa. Note that the *degrees* of terminating Elliott waves correlate with the varying extremes in dividend yield. Cycle degree extremes have produced over- and undervaluation at about 3% and 6.5% yield respectively, while Supercycle degrees have produced more extreme figures. Now look at 1999, where the dividend yield for the DJIA is only 1.5%, the lowest in the history of the data. Since we have record of a Supercycle overvaluation on the chart (in 1929), and since this one is higher, *it must reflect a developing top of higher than Supercycle degree*, i.e., one of at least Grand Supercycle degree.

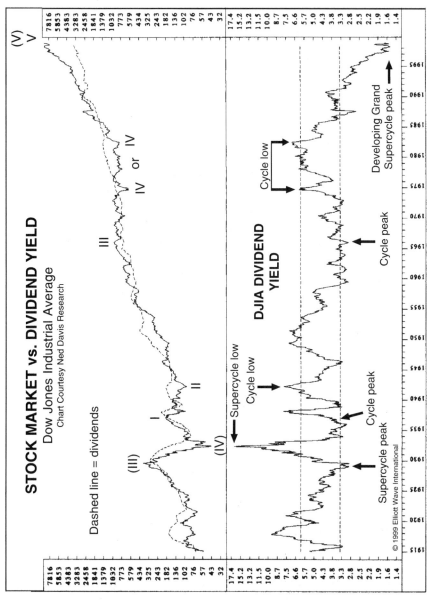

Figure 10

Figure 11 shows a similar measure, from two complex perspectives simultaneously. The X axis reflects the yield available from AAA corporate bonds as compared to the yield available from the S&P 400 Industrials, while the Y axis reflects stock prices as compared to the book values of the underlying corporations. Perhaps even more definitively than Figure 10, Figure 11 shows an overvaluation today that dramatically dwarfs anything seen this century, which covers all degrees through Supercycle. Once again, therefore, the current valuation *must reflect a developing top of at least*

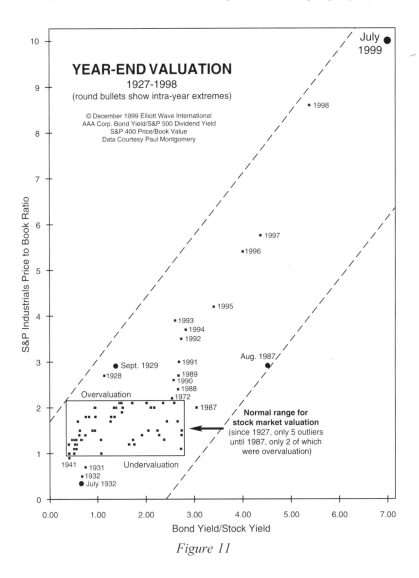

Figure 11

Grand Supercycle degree. By all such pertinent measures, our labeling in Figure 9 is correct.

Although statistics proving this point are sparse, we can make a case that the "fundamental" background of what we have labeled waves (III) and (V) in Figure 9 support the labeling as well. Wave (III) had better GNP figures and better conditions attending production than did wave (V). For example, in the former time, there were essentially no taxes, while since 1932, taxes have soared to take 50% of people's income (then more upon death). Though tentatively, we speculate also that the ability of producers to plow nearly 100% of their profits back into the companies in the 1859-1929 period must have attended a better technical picture in the advance-decline line for that time, as businesses had a better chance of succeeding.

Is Long-Term Forecasting Possible with the Wave Principle?

Long-term forecasting with the Wave Principle has produced some remarkable results. In December 1979, *The Elliott Wave Theorist* assessed the patterns revealed on the graphs of inflation-related phenomena. In recognizing the end of a long-term impulsive process, EWT came to this conclusion:

> The incredible conjunction of "fives" in different markets [gold, silver, interest rates, bonds, and commodities] all seem to point to the same conclusion: The world is about to begin a phase of general disinflation [i.e., decelerating inflation]. As I see it, a pattern of several disinflationary years leading to a deflationary trend later on would be a perfect scenario for the Elliott outlook for stocks. A gradual disinflation would create an optimistic mood in the country and lead to the conclusion that we may have finally licked the inflation problem. This sentiment would support a bull market in stocks for several years until the snowballing forces of deflation began to take over. At that point, a major deflationary crash would be impossible to avert, and the Grand Supercycle correction would be underway.
>
> —December 1979, *The Elliott Wave Theorist*

This forecast was printed in the January 1980 issue of *Commodities* (now *Futures*) magazine. The rate of inflation peaked that month, and the script described above has played out (albeit over a much longer time than originally anticipated) ever since. Figures 12 and 13 show the outcome.

Figure 12

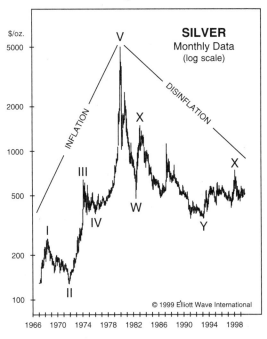

Figure 13

In 1982, *The Elliott Wave Theorist* assessed the DJIA, this time recognizing the end of a long-term *corrective* process. Figure 14 shows the forecast that was issued with the analysis calling for an advance in stock prices of Cycle degree, which is exactly what has unfolded, though once again, it has been a much bigger Cycle degree advance than originally expected.

As these and many other examples show, the Wave Principle is not only a useful tool for anticipating major changes in financial trends but probably the only reliable tool for this purpose. Moreover, as the past two decades demonstrate, the economic, monetary and social results of major changes in waves are tangible and important. As a whole, then, the preceding overview of today's stock market with respect to Cycle, Supercycle and Grand Supercycle degree waves should be taken for substantially more than an academic exercise.

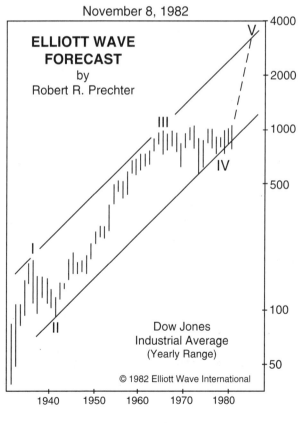

Figure 14

Manias and Their Aftermaths

Should we care that the stock market is making a Grand-Supercycle top? Pundits tell us, "The stock market always comes back." Well, many stocks have indeed come back during the course of the Supercycle degree uptrend since 1932 and even the Grand Supercycle degree uptrend since 1784. But even within those times, bear markets as small as Cycle degree have caused many companies to go bankrupt, their names forgotten. As with every other social effect of wave dynamics, the effect is proportional to the degree of the wave. How big a wave are we expecting?

On rare occasions, a financial market will be subject to a mania. A mania is a rare event whose aspects include historic overvaluation and broad public participation. Figures 10 and 11 reveal that today's stock market is historically overvalued. Statistics on stock ownership reflect the broadest public stock participation perhaps in the history of man. As the examples shown in Figure 15 reveal, manias are always more than fully retraced. This crucial piece of information is in full concordance with the fact that the Supercycle wave from 1932 is a *fifth* wave and must be mostly retraced by the normal course of Elliott-wave development. This means that the mania, which dates from 1982, will be more than fully retraced by the next bear market. Specifically, the next bear market will take the DJIA below 777. According to our only relevant data, most stocks do *not* come back after they have been subject to manic overvaluation. At least, that was the experience of the London stock exchange following the South Sea Bubble, a stock mania that peaked in 1720. A scant two years later, over half the stocks that were trading at the top were no longer even listed.

Manias are highly damaging to the economy because of the breadth and depth of public participation. As a mania progresses, prosperity itself becomes dependent upon the continued rise of a manic market. When the market finally turns down, so does prosperity. It is particularly instructive to note that the Great Depression began in September 1929, the same month as the great stock price reversal following the near-mania of the Roaring 'Twenties. This immediate response is in contrast to the typical multi-month lag between smaller stock market tops and ensuing economic contractions. Because the mania of the 1980s-1990s has been far greater than that of the 1920s, its reversal will have far more severe economic results than the reversal of 1929. In other words, the next depression will be deeper than that of 1933.

Famous Market Manias And Their Aftermaths 1600-1999

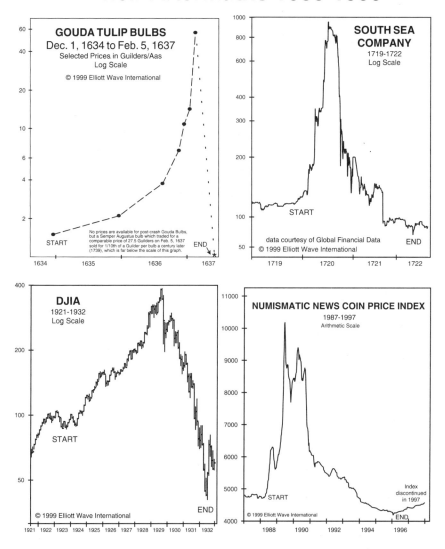

Figure 15a

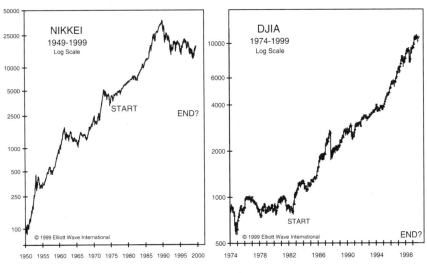

Figure 15b

Exactly When?

Whether the Grand Supercycle bear market has already begun is impossible to say, but the evidence that a major, indeed historic, downturn is developing has piled up to the ceiling. The economic and social effects of this bear market will be so severe that anyone not prepared will be devastated. It is better to be early, even years early, than one day too late.

[*Note: This paper was also delivered as a speech to the annual New Orleans Conference in November 1999. You are welcome to hear this presentation on Elliott Wave International's website at* www.elliottwave.com/viewfromthetop *and then click on "New Orleans speech, 1999."*]

*Battling Euphoria in the
Post-Peak Topping Process*

Questions & Answers With
Bob Prechter

conducted by market commentator and author Franklin Sanders

Q: I figure you have a lot of new subscribers who might like to get oriented. As a long-time reader myself, I wouldn't mind a refresher course. I also want some input on where the market is right now. Can we have a chat?

> **A:** Go for it.

Q: Let's talk about the Wave Principle first. Various researchers have made the case that markets unfold in patterns, but no one has yet suggested a reason for them. Can you summarize in just a few words *why* markets move in patterns?

> **A:** Here's the way I see it. Many people desire to belong to and be accepted by the group. Many people also have a tendency to let others think for them in fields they find intellectually difficult. These traits serve to make their unconscious minds dominate their conscious minds, especially in emotionally charged social settings. When the market panics, for instance, most investors are not panicking individually in isolation, but in response to the panic of others. The same is true of their buying, but that is a slower process and therefore less obvious. When the unconscious mind dominates, it does not do so randomly — as that would mean no thought at all — but in patterns peculiar to it. Those patterns show up in price movement and reflect the Wave Principle. I presented a lot of evidence for this conclusion in *The Wave Principle of Human Social Behavior*.

Q: What do you advise people to do who want to learn to use the Wave Principle?

A: The first thing to do is to start watching market plots closely. Label and channel the real-time movements according to the Wave Principle. You'll gain confidence immediately if the market is in a major impulse rather than a correction. That is when I was fortunate enough to begin, so I saw what was happening quickly. Corrections are more varied and difficult. Yet even corrections usually *contain* impulse waves, so you should observe plenty of them before long.

Q: How can I get the big picture?

A: You should obtain data as far back as possible. The more information you have, the better. The perspective provided can be invaluable. The approaching juncture in the stock market is an example. The expected change in trend is of very large degree, a fact that would not be understood without three centuries of back data.

Q: Should an analyst rely on other market indicators when coming to an analytical conclusion about the market?

A: No approach, including Elliott, provides an assured scenario. However, Elliott analysis does provide a list of possible outcomes in order of their probability, which is a lot. Still, you must accept that sometimes a lower probability count will turn out correct; that's what "lower probability" means. Sentiment and momentum readings, along with other guidelines of wave behavior, can help you weigh the possible outcomes properly. Our *Elliott Wave Principle* book describes how psychology, speed of price change and breadth behave at certain times in the structure, which is useful to know when you're trying to identify the market's position in that structure. To avoid the biggest mistake that people (including me) make, never label the market simply because of the way indicators look. They can look that way for a long time.

Q: The Wave Principle reflects all degrees of trend at once. Can a count at Subminuette degree affect your Primary degree count?

A: Each degree is relevant to patterns one or two degrees higher. Here's an example. Suppose I think the market should be rising in a third wave, but on the smaller degree, the rise to a new high is choppy, while breadth is poor and the rate of change slow. I would revise the count to label the advance as wave B of a flat correction for wave two.

A Subminuette degree event could affect my opinion at Primary degree, but only as a component of patterns building up to Intermediate degree. Every decision point ultimately comes down to *some* threshold at the smallest degree.

Q: Under the Wave Principle, what is the most important thing to watch other than price?

A: Volume. Generally increasing volume on a fifth wave below Primary degree, for instance, means that the wave will extend. Light volume in a supposed third wave means it's not a third wave. Both of these situations present invaluable information. Remember, it happens at many degrees, so there is a lot of information to assess.

Q: O.K., let's switch to today's stock market. You were so bullish for many years. Are you comfortable with your grim long-term forecast of a Grand Supercycle degree reversal?

A: Well, I don't put the words "grim" and "forecast" together. What is coming is just reality. It will be grim to the unprepared and life-enhancing to those properly positioned. You could say the forecast for the bull market I made in 1982 was grim to short sellers. The point of the forecast is to make what is coming a profitable experience, or at minimum a safe one, for you as an individual.

Q: Can you summarize your long-term outlook for stocks and bonds, the dollar, gold, inflation and economic growth?

A: I think the rise in U.S. stocks is in a terminal phase and faces a historic trend change. Most stock markets worldwide are likely to follow suit. Major stock declines have always led to recessions or depressions, and this time should be no different. Social unrest will follow in many areas of the world. The bond market is not a haven, as it topped out in 1998. The quality of investment debt overall is the lowest in human history, and bond investors will have to pay for an error in judgment. I have been bullish from time to time on gold and silver in the near term, but their bear market is not quite over yet. Over the next ten years, the biggest risk we face is deflation. Economists are cheering the low inflation rate, but the long-term trend in the rate of inflation is akin to where it was in 1929, so it is not good news. Later in the deflationary process, precious metals will be the single best investment. We are watching carefully to be able to identify that time.

Q: Where will the Dow be when the decline is over, and when do you think that will happen?

A: Every financial mania in history has been followed by a collapse that takes prices to below where they were when the uptrend began, which in the current case is Dow 777 in 1982. I do not know when it will bottom because we will be dealing with a major corrective process that could last a century. It will be a great fourth wave, balancing the second wave, a bear market that lasted from 1720 to 1784. The first major low should occur in 2003-2004. I outlined the entire scenario in *At the Crest*, but it is too speculative to detail here.

Q: Aren't there some stock markets, in Asia, for instance, that you believe are closer to a bottom than a top?

A: They are staging partial recoveries within bear markets. The full retracement of the Nikkei's mania has yet to be completed.

Q: You have anticipated these events for quite some time, at a huge opportunity cost. Where did your calculations go wrong?

A: It has been frustrating. In 1982 and 1983, I described the coming mania, which would be "like 1929, 1968 and 1973 combined...indicators will give sell signal after sell signal, and the market will just keep on going." It was an insight only "Elliott" could provide. Unfortunately, I thought we would reach that point in no more than 8 years, which is actually on the long side for most of history's manias. But so far, it has lasted 18 years! If I weren't such an optimist, I would think that this means the top is even bigger than Grand Supercycle. By the way, I would add that the idea of "opportunity cost" is valid only if someone gets out at a higher level. Most people won't. The gunslingers who have ignored historic overvaluation to "make money" in the past decade will not get out for the down move. Their financial dreams will dissolve. Would you rather be that person, or the one who cashed out early and avoided getting caught up in the mania?

Q: What about the notion of "lower probability?" Do you think the fact that your predictions have not happened yet might mean that you have misinterpreted even the long-term the wave count?

A: The Wave Principle allows plenty of alternate interpretations, but market conditions and patterns such as those in place today have clear implications, and those implications will be borne out. It is only a matter of when, not if.

Q: Investors' exuberance, irrational or otherwise, for buying stocks is being sustained partly by a belief that traditional notions about company valuations and economic cycles no longer apply. "This time it's different," the bulls cry. Why are they necessarily wrong?

A: "Necessarily" is a good word because the widespread acceptance of the idea that economic cycles are dead answers the question of why we have economic cycles. People's beliefs about trends are not scientific but emotional. When markets have gyrated, they believe in cycles. When they go down for a long time, they believe in doomsday. When they go up for a long time, they believe that cycles are dead and the only possible direction is up. If people were different in terms of being intellectually independent and commonly expecting trend changes, then financial markets would be far more stable.

Q: If the society and its leaders are careful, can we avoid the bear market?

A: Being "careful" now cannot avert the coming social change. Society and its leaders have been uncareful for a long time, and their actions will have consequences. Still, individuals can take steps to insure the safety of their own capital and later, their personal safety as well.

Q: What would you say to a cynic who finds it odd that your work would coincide with the greatest shift in the course of human progress in 200 years and concludes that the only thing this opinion really demonstrates is the need for market analysts to feel as though they're living at a critical moment in history?

A: It's a sophisticated point about human nature. I have made the point myself, in other contexts, such as in discussing "end of the world" people. When Y2K was supposed to mark the end of civilization, I said to ignore it. [Bob's Bulletin Board, 9/4/97: "As for the millennium bug, I believe the free market will solve the problem and that it will prove to be pretty much a non-event for most people."] Whether it's earthquakes, pole shifts, giant meteors, Armageddon, overpopulation, the ozone layer or whatever, many people seem to be able to justify believing passionately that the world is about to end a few months from now. But the stock market always falls a long way before social strife erupts, so I was quite sure that Y2K would be a non-event. Now, back to the Elliott wave outlook. If the cynic doesn't bother to look at the patterns and has no historical context, then his perspective makes mine look psychologically self-serving. However, if he were to read all the Elliott wave material from R.N. Elliott through Charles Collins, Hamilton Bolton, A.J. Frost and myself, he would understand that our reading of the long-term wave pattern has been consistent for sixty years, anticipating the juncture that we now face. It has been anything but an "end of the world" stance. We've been mostly bullish, in fact, super-bullish, except for 1966-1974, which was the wave IV correction, and in the past decade as we await the end of wave (V) of a two-century uptrend. Finally, I would say, "Watch what happens."

Q: Does the fact that pollution, overpopulation, AIDS and tin-pot dictators are still with us mean that things could get a whole lot better before the top?

A: There is always a mix of good and bad in the worldwide social picture. The question is, what is the balance? Today, on average, there is less pollution (due to the collapse of European Communism), more widespread peace, more high-paying jobs and fewer tin-pot dictatorships than ever before. And those points merely scratch the surface. People don't realize they are living in a Golden Age until it's over. Whatever one might view as negatives now will appear as nothing at the bottom of the next depression.

Q: Do you think history will treat you kindly?

A: Most people will not be paying as much attention to the stock market after it falls, so in a few years, most of today's investors will not care who predicted what. Their focus will be on other things.

Q: You sound like you are counting on many investors holding on all the way through a bear market. Would it be right to guess that you think this will happen because so many people invest through funds?

A: No. It's *always* been true. But there is one aspect of the mutual fund craze that is worth a comment. After the 1987 crash, investors found that they could not stand the pain of taking the blame for their own losses. So they abdicated responsibility by handing over their funds to managers. Now, ironically, they can stand a much larger loss psychologically because IT WON'T BE THEIR FAULT. They can rail at the apparent stupidity of managers instead of their own naivete. Ultimately, all novices sell at lower prices; in fact, they usually sell near the bottom. Many sell shortly after the final bottom, thinking they have gotten a rally to sell on.

Q: OK, I get the picture, and I can handle this topping period. But what about the coming bear market? How bad will our experience be?

A: Even a bear as large as a Grand Supercycle will *not* be doomsday. These are just social trends. You as an individual can avoid the difficulties. For those who had steady income or large savings, the 1930s were a fantastic time. Everything was cheap. Just make sure you're not caught in the wrong country, as there will be wars and dictatorships a few decades from now in areas you would never guess.

Q: So what should investors do, especially less sophisticated ones who don't want to sell short or trade derivatives?

A: In deflations and depressions, cash is king. Make sure you have a safe currency and a safe haven for it. Then plan what you will buy at the bottom. Finally, I suggest that you invert the stock and bond market charts and watch the value of your cash rise in a long-term bull market.

Q: Are there currently any significant Fibonacci relationships in the stock market that might indicate a reversal is at hand?

A: Over the years, I have anticipated a number of long-term Fibonacci relationships in the DJIA. Some, like the 1987 high, coincided with market reversals. Those in the 1990s have not — except briefly — as the Dow has continued to rise. However, in a historically overvalued market that is staggering under ever-compounding technical indications of an approaching reversal, I think we have to stay focused on the single most important question, which is when and where that reversal will take place. I do have some charts that I've been keeping an eye on. Want to see them?

Q: Sure!

A: OK; just remember, you asked for them. Here's a study I've just completed:

Fibonacci Relationships in Cycle Wave V

Price

The history of the DJIA shows a web of Fibonacci multiples in terms of both price values and price distances. It is probable that the greatest top of all time will also be in Fibonacci relationship to the structure that preceded it.

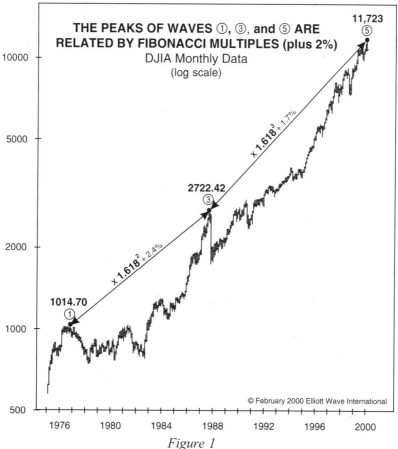

Figure 1

Figure 1 illustrates that within wave V, the peak values of the three impulse waves (①, ③ and ⑤) are related by Fibonacci multiples at the January high of 11,723. Wave ③ topped at a level that is **2.618** (1.618^2) times the peak of wave ①. Wave ⑤, if it ended on January 14, topped at a level that is **4.236** (1.618^3) times the peak of wave ③. In each case, the Dow traveled an extra 2% (+ or – 0.3%) before topping.

The recent high is also a Fibonacci **11.09** (1.618^5) times the 1966 high of 995.15 *and* a Fibonacci **29.03** (1.618^7) times the 1929 high of 381.17, each plus 7%. Figure 2 shows these relationships.

It is curious that for each Fibonacci ratio power involved, the market appears to travel an additional 1%. It adds about 2% to 1.618^2 and 7% to 1.618^7.

For the record, market watchers Barclay T. Leib, Terry McCormick and Jean Comeau have made similar observations about the 11,500s level using somewhat different approaches.

Figure 2

Next Level

If the Dow exceeds the January 14 high, it will likely top near 13,000, for reasons detailed in the January 1999 EWT. [See the bottom chart in Section Two, page 160. — Ed.] Figures 3 through 5 suggest that it should still occur this year.

Time

Figure 3 shows that the great wave V mania has unfolded in two stages lasting a Fibonacci **13** years each. The first lasted from 1974 to 1987 and the other from 1987 to 2000. Recall that the 1987 high met the upside price and time target published in *Elliott Wave Principle* nearly a decade earlier. The 1987 crash seemed to have "reset" the market, as from that point, it has undergone a second advance of the same duration. A rough time parallelism would allow for a top any time in the year 2000.

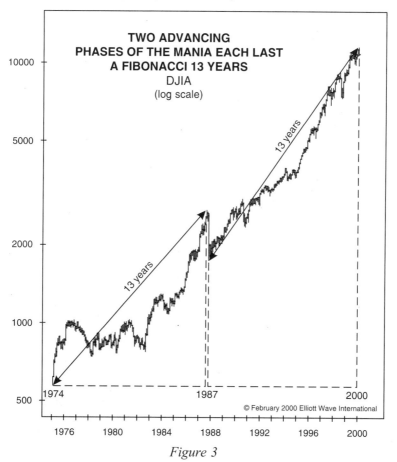

Figure 3

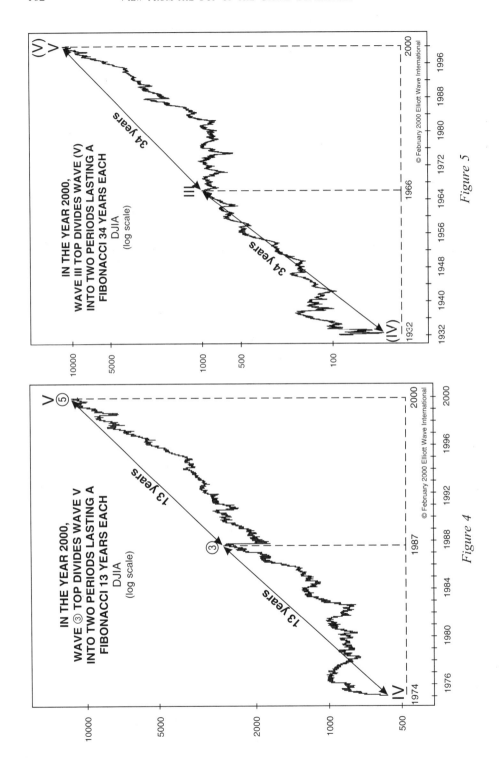

Figure 5

Figure 4

Take a look at Figures 4 and 5. Observe that the time event occurring this year at Cycle degree is simultaneously occurring at Supercycle degree. Figure 4 shows that the 1987 high, which is the high of wave ③, divides Cycle wave V into two periods lasting a Fibonacci **13** years each in the year 2000. Figure 5 shows that the 1966 high, which is the high of wave III, divides Supercycle wave (V) into two periods lasting a Fibonacci **34** years each in the year 2000. [So the peak of wave three in both cases is the point at which the entire wave subdivides into two equal Fibonacci time periods.]

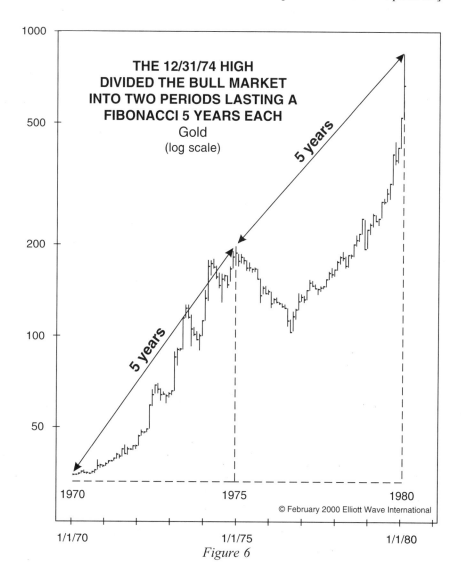

Figure 6

There is at least one notable precedent for a peak dividing a major uptrend into two Fibonacci durations. The major advance in gold began near New Year's Day of 1970 and ended near New Year's Day of 1980. The mid-trend peak occurred on New Year's Day of 1975, dividing the bull market into two periods lasting a Fibonacci **5** years each, as shown in Figure 6.

Some fine points for Elliotters: The mid-trend high in gold was not wave III but wave B of IV. Wave B of an expanded flat wave four is the price high *associated* with the end of wave three. The low in 1970 was wave II, but it was the low of the period; wave I started at a higher level — by $0.50 — in actual prices because the price of gold was previously fixed by the government.

The situation in the DJIA today is more impressive, as the same event is potentially resolving *simultaneously at two major degrees of trend*. At Cycle degree (Figure 4), the two time lines also form a *single trendline*, another interesting coincidence that we also see in the gold chart (Figure 6). These observations may come to naught, or they may end up revealing an aspect of wave pattern formation that we can add to the catalog of guidelines.

The Elliott Wave Financial Forecast
Special Report

February 25, 2000

Deflation and the New Economy

by Peter Kendall, Elliott Wave International

"...with growing optimism, they gave birth to a foolish idea called the 'New Economic Era.' That notion spread over the whole country. We were assured that we were in a new period where the old laws of economics no longer applied."

—The Memoirs of Herbert Hoover

At the end of Supercycle (III) in the 1920s, the talk of a new era escalated with Hoover's election in 1928 and continued until the crash of October 1929. Figure 1, depicting the number of major references to the "New Economy" since 1985, illustrates this same phenomenon recurring, this time on a Grand-Supercycle scale. The modern notion has been widespread for more than five full years and for the past year has been accelerating at an unprecedented rate. In 1999, the number of articles in major publications focusing on the new economy rose 2.4 times from a record in 1998. In January 2000, the annualized rate was 7 times that of 1998. As discussed below, it is no coincidence that this acceleration comes as evidence of price deflation has mounted. The February issue of EWFF showed that falling prices hit many parts of the world in 1999. As late as November, there was speculation that global prices might actually be down for the year.

At the Crest of the Tidal Wave first identified the connection between the gathering deflationary storm and the belief in a New Economy. "The true threat today is not inflation, but deflation," *At the Crest* said. "There is no hint of any such crisis on the horizon because economists are unanimous in their identification of slowing money supply expansion and moderated price gains as the best imaginable news for long-term economic growth." Since then, the New Economy has grown into an elaborate myth. It reflects the positive psychology of the extensive bull market in social mood, which serves as cover for the dangerous transition from inflation to

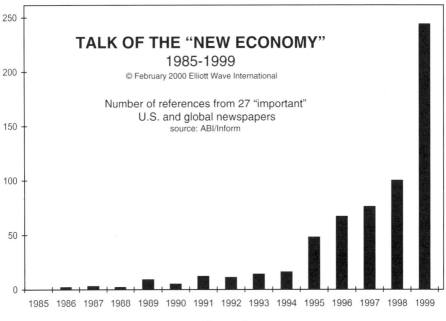

Figure 1

deflation. R.N. Elliott said, "It is a well known fact that prosperity and depression follow each other in cycles." It is a reality that most people admit only at market bottoms. That is why a search of 27 major newspapers finds no references to a "new economy" in 1980. As late as 1985, when the bull market entered Intermediate (3) of Primary ③, there were still no such references. Even in the middle of the 1990s, many of the references were qualified and others rightfully warned that the very idea of it was a sign of an overly enthusiastic social psychology. The dramatic quickening in the new era drumbeat recalls the drunken revelry in Troy as the Greeks' famous wooden horse was accepted inside the gates of the citadel.[1] The more exaggerated and insistent the reports of the triumph of the New Economy and the death of the business cycle become, the more emphatically they reveal the hidden fact that the economy is back where it was in the fall of 1929, at the cusp of a great deflationary downturn.

Public Enemy No. 2

The monetary parallel to the 1920s is very much intact. The rate-of-change charts for the producer and consumer price indexes shown in Figure

2 are updated from *At the Crest*. They show that the disinflationary pattern of the 1980s and 1990s continues to track that of the 1920s. As *At the Crest* noted, "Each burst of reflationary pressure since 1982 has been less intense. Lessening intensity is a classic precursor to trend change." The dotted lines mark an even longer "slowing of the peak rates of price change over this entire century. This long-term slowing implies a trend reversal not just of Supercycle degree, then, but of Grand Supercycle degree." Despite this long slide to the doorstep of deflation, there is virtually no recognition, let alone fear, of the potential for an outright decline in prices. If anything, the mentality discussed at the very start of *At the Crest*'s "Monetary Outlook" is more intense than ever: "The most widely held beliefs with regard to the future course of national monetary affairs are (1) that inflation is the number one economic threat and (2) that the Federal Reserve is in full control of monetary expansion and contraction." *At the Crest* challenges these assumptions, saying, "the first is a case of fighting the last war," and "the second is pure mythology." As the leading public figure in a fight against an enemy that has been in retreat for 20 years, Alan Greenspan's status has risen to that of a brilliant shaman. In a classic display of his powerful magic, the Fed Chairman recently characterized the economy's performance as "the best in a half century" and then warned that "inflation remains a threat to the economic good times." The feverish public interest with which Greenspan's message of "lurking" inflation was received and the widening discrepancy between inflationary anxieties and economic realities suggests, however, that the standing monetary assumptions have reached their breaking point. The state of psychology on these issues signals that a sustained break of the zero-line in CPI and PPI growth is imminent.

The Miracle of Modern Productivity

The intense social focus on the "last war" also helps explain how a Grand-Supercycle-degree rationalization called the New Economy could be constructed around the symptoms of an encroaching deflation. To understand how it has developed and why it will soon dissolve, let's look at one of the central justifications behind much of the belief, the big surge in productivity. A deluge of recent articles on the subject includes a lengthy *Washington Post* study that proclaims, "New numbers provide dramatic confirmation that the new economy not only exists but continues to thrive. The new economy is about what can be done and what can be dreamed." "Dreamed" is the key word here because it reveals the euphoric emotional

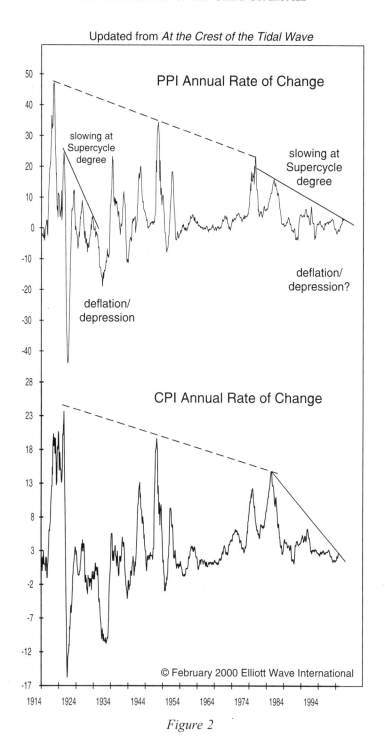

Figure 2

tone that underlies all of these stories. Similar missives are literally daily events now. Here are two more examples from this past Monday. The one at the top is from the publisher of *Forbes* and the one below it is from a *Business Week* editorial.

Can this benign environment last? Any history buff would say no. But the Internet offers the possibility, once slim but now becoming more probable by the day, that the good times *can* run a long while.
—*Forbes*, February 21, 2000

Is the growth in U.S. productivity accelerating? Recent figures suggest it may be, and the implications are vast: Living standards could rise faster, profits may increase further, economic growth might be higher, the budget surplus might grow bigger.
—*Business Week*,
February 21, 2000

Business Week's faith in a productivity-induced boom borders on a religious conviction. Every week it produces "More Evidence" in the form of recent conversions. In January, it was the former chief economic advisor to the President who said, " I am rapidly becoming a New Economy convert. Productivity gains from technology have altered the economic playing field." In the January 31 "New Economy" cover story shown above, *Business Week* argued that the "innovation factor" is one big reason "the New Economy bandwagon" is very likely going global. But the story also betrays the media's blindness to the evidence of deflation when it touches on the elimination of natural boundaries to competition. "Historically, it has taken years, if not decades, for even the most important technological innovations to spread across national borders. Now, an engineer in China, say, can log on to the Internet and have immediate access to the treasure trove of data on U.S. web sites." The bull-market bias blinds writers to the fact that the Internet has the potential to be as dangerous in some ways as it is productive in others. For more than a year, we have monitored the media for a glimmer of realization that innovation could actually contribute to the deflationary process. In that time, we have seen just one small hint of it. That was in *The Economist* shortly after the renewed Asian collapse in late 1998. Even in that case, however, the essay concluded that America will "not suffer from malign deflation" because "productivity-driven deflation is beneficial."

If that were true, however, the early 1930s would have seen a continuation of the growth and euphoria of the 1920s. In *Business Cycles* (1939), Joseph Schumpeter pointed out, "the Depression acted as an efficiency expert," increasing output per man hour 20% from 1929 to 1932. Schumpeter, an Austrian economist, was one of the all-time great business cycle theorists. He would surely contest the notion that technology can be counted on to soften the blow of deflation. After years of study, Schumpeter concluded that "innovation" itself played the central role in the "wave-like alternation" between prosperity and depression. In a classic swing from prosperity to depression, the downtrend begins when "profits are eliminated" and wealth generation and capital accumulation cease. This time around, however, excitement over the Internet's prospects has run so high (Internet stock investors who cannot handle losses "are wimps," says the author of the article below) that profits may not be achieved until *after* the deflationary washout. There are several major reasons to believe that downswing is now rolling in. Let's explore them one by one.

The Case for
LOSING MONEY

It's a running joke among Net entrepreneurs. Venture capitalists won't fund you unless you can prove your company will lose $450 million in the first six months – otherwise they figure you're not ambitious enough. Profits? Oh, please. Tell them your business model is so extensible that you'll scale up first and monetize later. E-commerce leaders are right to keep spending – even if that means more losses.

—*Business Week*, February 7, 2000

An Unprecedented Capital Explosion

An investment frenzy often precedes deflation. Clearly, a speculative frenzy has engulfed the dot-com world. The IPO boom of 1999 is a perfect representation of the kind of climactic rush that Schumpeter noted typically occurred at the onset of big downturns. In addition to the $68 billion raised in IPOs in 1999, which was 40% higher than any year on record, a vast mushroom cloud of venture capital has formed over the entire high-tech sector. In 1999, venture capitalists invested $48.2 billion, an amount that surpassed the prior three years combined. Venture firms are now so "awash in money that many partners have no time to do anything more than drop by for board meetings." This scene has unfolded outside the U.S. as well. "European Venture Funds Throw Wads of Money at Internet Start-Ups, Too," says one recent headline. In India, South Korea and Japan, the stories are much the same. The rate of growth in this boom is typical of a pre-deflation investment frenzy.

Venture Capitalists 'R' Us

Now, Everyone Is Diving In, Seeing No-Lose Situation

—The Wall Street Journal, *February 22, 2000*

Venture Firms' U.S. Investments Set Records for Quarter and Year

It is no secret that venture capitalists invested a lot of money in 1999. But the surge turned out to be a tsunami. Driven by the dot-com frenzy, venture-capital investments in U.S. companies more than tripled in the fourth quarter and more than doubled for the entire year, according to [a venture capital researcher].

The boom reflects the frantic rate of company formation, powered by low barriers to entry in Internet businesses, and prospects that communications technology can reshape entertainment, commerce and corporate business practices. "It is like standing under a waterfall trying to take a drink," said a partner at a large venture firm.

—*The Wall Street Journal*
February 7, 2000

Cyberspace Merges with the Mainstream

Another reason to expect deflation is that mainstream firms are moving in on the turf of the Internet pioneers. Schumpeter said that it is not the profits themselves but the commitment of "more and more firms" to the businesses and methods of the future that creates the bust. We observe this movement in everything from Time Warner's willingness to be acquired by Internet upstart AOL to the focus of *Business Week*'s more recent Internet cover stories. The latest ones profile the Internet *response* of firms like Merrill Lynch, IBM and a myriad of conventional retailers. On January 14, *The Wall Street Journal* reported, "The real world is merging with the virtual world." A few days later, it added, "The entire 'brick and mortar' economy is turning into a 'click and mortar' economy, as traditional companies turn to the web for new ways of distribution, or to fight upstarts from the Internet." Schumpeter noted that an emerging deflationary downswing gets down to business when companies effect a broad-based "adaptation to the new things created" during the boom. Together, the recent articles on the next page form a classic portrait of just such a transformation to a brutally competitive business environment.

A Web of Collapsing Prices

Expanding the case for deflation is the Internet's potential for price destruction. As the August 1998 issue of EWT noted, "The web is a massive engine for falling prices." This dark side has clearly started to surface in many forms. "Pricing isn't what it used to be, thanks to auctions and reverse auctions...Consumers can increasingly use the web to drive harder bargains." Many "computer distributors and other marketers" now see the web as a "frightening new world in which price alone — not service or quality or brand — dictates who wins a sale." From the sea of red ink that is the Internet, a horrifying four-letter word is surfacing more and more. "For [Internet] start-ups, free may be the only way to go," notes a consultant. "The danger of charging for your software is that a maker of a competing software product is going to come along with $30 million in venture money and just give it away." Doug Casey points out in a recent issue of his ever-insightful *International Speculator* (available at www.dougcasey.com or 1217 St. Paul St., Baltimore, Md., 410-234-0691) that there is no way to turn back this technologically driven assault on prices. "On the net a competitor can be anywhere; so prices will start falling to the lowest levels possible not just in a given community or a given country, but in the world."

Even Offline Publications Try Giving It Away

A co-founder of TheStreet.com, admits that he got it painfully wrong. He thought his financial news service could charge $99.95 a year for access to its site. He now realizes that Internet users "won't pay for news, and they're adamant about it and they're angry" if they have to pay. And the idea that information should be free is increasingly popular in the offline world as well.

—*The New York Times*
January 27, 2000

Japan Inc. at Last Embracing Internet

Japan Inc. embraces the Internet economy? Such a notion might seem strange, given the failure so far of the nation's planning mandarins and its corporate elite to pull the world's second-largest economy out of its decade-long economic funk. But perhaps the thought isn't so strange after all.

Across much of Asia high-tech startups have captured the attention of savvy venture capitalists and forward-looking corporate dealmakers. Governments have embraced these new engines of economic growth, providing additional seed capital, helping develop alternative stock market "exits" for such high risk investments and deregulating the investment and trade barriers that allow these startups to thrive.

Japanese prime minister Obuchi made it clear in his opening address to the nation's parliament in early February that if he can help it, Japan will not lag behind its neighbors in the high-tech venture capital arena. He outlined his government's determination to pour money into the nation's so-called "info-communications" infrastructure, which includes telecom services and broadcasting, and into high-tech Internet startups, telecom and new industries, such as biotechnology, environmental industries and medical and welfare-related services.

A surge in capital spending driven by a much-needed technological upgrade will be the impetus behind the upcycle. New startups will force existing players to start investing in Internet technology. A latecomer to the information revolution, Japan will now do what it does best: catch up.
— *The Daily Deal*, February 8, 2000

WHY THE PRODUCTIVITY REVOLUTION WILL SPREAD

Old-line companies, from Royal/Shell Group to Honeywell to General Electric, are pushing hard to move the Net-driven productivity revolution from the fab land to the heartland. "Think about the implications across all industries," says [the] founder of a Menlo Park, Calif., consultancy. "We're talking trillions of dollars in productivity gains when all is said and done."

"Everyone in every sector is facing a marketplace that is just relentless on costs."

Suddenly, the Internet has gone from a threat to established industrial age companies to a tool with nearly unlimited potential. If used wisely, it could keep this economic engine humming for some time to come.
—Business Week, *February 14, 1999*

So called Old Economy companies such as banks, retailers and old-style telecommunications firms (the bricks), have spent the past year or two beefing up their New Economy assets (the clicks). And now, they are confronting the next hurdle: getting the market to recognize the value of their Internet operations, wireless-phone operations or venture-capital investments. This rush comes despite the slump in stocks such as Barnes & Noble Inc.'s Barnes&Noble.com or Donaldson, Lufkin & Jenrette Inc.'s DLJdirect Inc. – *The Wall Street Journal*, February 8, 2000

"There is a lot of technology at risk now because of all the new stuff," [an economic strategist] says. "But that's what makes this so exciting. The new [technology firms] make the old ones compete harder." —USA Today, *February 10, 2000*

Sporting Goods Firms At Last Leaving E-Commerce Sidelines

—The Atlanta Constitution, *February 9, 2000*

It's come to this: The Internet is transforming even lowly utilities.
—The Wall Street Journal,
February 8, 2000

The Rest of a Very Old Story

The groundwork for deflationary spiral is in place. Sometimes, as they marvel at all the "productivity growth," new paradigm writers even borrow Schumpeter's famous phrase about the "churn of creative destruction." In time, there are several more Schumpeterisms that will be revisited. These include the "elimination of what is incapable of adaptation," the "reorganization of economic life," "remodeling the system of value" and the "liquidation of indebtedness." These are what the new era is really about. The parabolic rise in references to the New Economy, the IPO boom, the mainstream movement to the Internet and the new downward pressure on prices suggest that, in the not so distant future, we will be hearing about these less glamorous aspects of the deflationary cycle.

A Long Build-Up Has Led to This Peak

Notice that all of the clips shown in this report are from within the last few weeks. The fact that we did not have to look far or wide for our evidence is a comment on the current environment. The transition to deflation is now moving at a rapid pace. However, the process has actually been unfolding in subtle but profound ways for two decades. Much of the early contraction was concealed in the form of corporate restructurings, buybacks and mergers that pumped up stock prices at the expense of revenues and companies' prospects for long-term growth. In a great article called "The Profit Illusion Game" from the Fall 1999 issue of *American Outlook* (available at 5395 Emerson Way, Indianapolis, IN 46226 or www.hudson.org), author Charles Parlato shows how the emasculation of book value, serial mergers, the stock repurchase game and earnings enhancements techniques have already contributed mightily to the prospects for deflation. The bull market's attendant accounting gimmicks will also get a lot more ink as the blinding light of the new era gives way to sober reflection and recrimination.

NOTES

[1] This prelude in which objections were gradually and then joyously overcome is also consistent with the Greek legend. Homer says that many Trojans wanted to run the hollow cavern of the wooden horse through with their swords and some wanted to "drag it to the peak and throw it off the rocks." According to *Bulfinch's Mythology*, Troy was fully apprised of the danger inherent in accepting the horse by a high priest who said, "What madness is this? For my part, I fear the Greeks even when they offer gifts." In time, however, "the tide of the people's feelings" turned against the priest, and they "no longer hesitated to regard the wooden horse as a sacred object, and prepared to introduce it with due solemnity into the city. This was done with songs and triumphal acclamations, and the day closed with festivity. In the night the armed men who were enclosed in the body of the horse opened the gates of the city to their friends, who had returned under the cover of night. The city was set on fire; the people, overcome with feasting and sleep, put to the sword, and Troy completely subdued."

April 2000

A *"Letter to the Editor" from*
Robert Prechter

Dear Editor,

I enjoy your theme of optimism, as it is sometimes an antidote to people's dabbling in bad philosophy. Nihilism, communism, relativism and authoritarianism get much of their power from pessimism. However, there is a difference between optimism and reason. Reason gives one cause to be optimistic about many things, but optimism is not a substitute for knowledge and reason. Usually you are on the right side of this one.

I have been reading your stock market optimism for quite some time without comment until now. In the April 2000 issue, you say, "The [recent stock market] losses were almost certainly temporary." This comment appears to be cavalier. It is immensely dangerous. Because reactions since 1982 have been brief is no reason to predict that the next one will be. You have to realize that in giving what amounts to investment advice, you are playing with your readers' life savings, their college plans and their retirement hopes. If you are wrong, they will suffer a lot. This kind of optimism is like telling someone suffering abdominal pain, "Your last four pains were nothing serious, so this one is almost certainly temporary." If you are not a doctor with specialized knowledge, you are endangering this person's life with "optimism."

I have studied the available 300+ years of stock market data and the accompanying social phenomena. The risk in holding stocks today is historically high. Perhaps the recent reaction is only a temporary pullback. Perhaps the person with symptoms of appendicitis will not die. However, these outcomes would be irrelevant to the fact that the proper course of action is to become properly informed about the field of one's concern before taking risk, not to make a flip observation and rely on it.

The WSJ article "False Negatives," which you cite, is more hindsight. I would call it worthless except that it is a big negative value, which is different. Articles like this never appear when they are useful, near bottoms.

This one appeared ten trading days from what is so far the all-time high in the Nasdaq Composite index. I think its writer will be guilty of ruining lives.

Today, everyone thinks he is a stock market expert. In 1980, everyone thought he was an expert on gold and inflation. All those experts are gone. The current crop will fade away as well. Don't let the nouveau geniuses give you their infection, which eventually will hurt both you and your subscribers. Remember, optimism flows from knowledge. One could have been optimistic in the early 1930s if he had avoided the crash and knew that recovery was on the way. However, if he had become absorbed in misguided optimism at the peak, he would have little left to spare at the bottom.

Anyway, that's my two cents. Take it or leave it, and keep doing the good job in all areas philosophic.

Robert R. Prechter, Jr.
President
Elliott Wave International

April 28, 2000

Deflation and Real Estate

When the NASDAQ collapsed on the announcement of the biggest monthly increase in the core inflation rate in five years, the media immediately latched onto the news as *the* reason for the big drop. Within two days, *The Wall Street Journal* had a big front-page story about "stirring" inflationary forces. However, there is no hard evidence of rising prices other than a two-month blip in the CPI in February-March. If there were a larger trend of rising prices for goods, the price of gold would have told us long before now.

The downward thrust shown in the long term chart of equity REITs, on the other hand, constitutes a signal that *de*flation and recession lie ahead. REITs are more sensitive to this potential because, as *At the Crest* stated, "Property is by far the worst market in which to speculate when the monetary cycle turns to deflation." At two-and-a-half years, the slump in REIT prices is already long enough to confirm at least part of *At the Crest*'s forecast: "The next economic contraction will not accompany simply another one-year setback in property prices. It will be a bigger decline in values than that of the 1930s." Obviously, however, there is a long way to go.

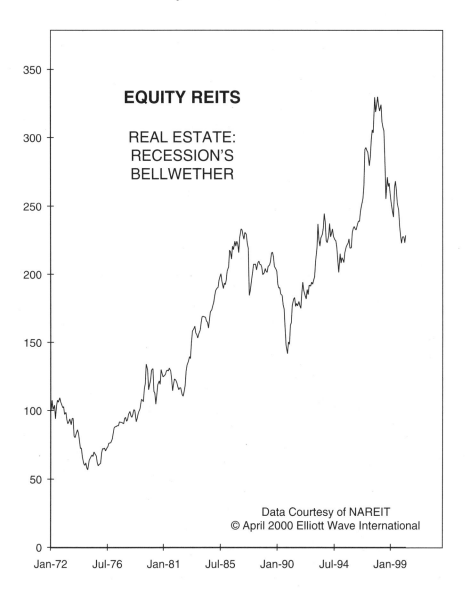

EQUITY REITS

REAL ESTATE:
RECESSION'S
BELLWETHER

Data Courtesy of NAREIT
© April 2000 Elliott Wave International

The Elliott Wave Financial Forecast

May 26, 2000

One Small Step for the Utilities...

by Peter Kendall and Steven Hochberg, Elliott Wave International

A stock market peak is a rolling series of upside non-confirmations. There is no moment of clarity when all stocks turn together and announce, "it's time to sell." The even distribution of arrows along the highs on the accompanying chart of the Dow depict a typical topping process. One by one, indicators and indexes have rolled over and started to fall. There is one important difference from the usual timing, however. This time, the process started all the way back in 1997. At two years and eight months, this stock market topping process is easily the longest on record. Along the way, it has established all the valuation records in the book (see **Valuation,**

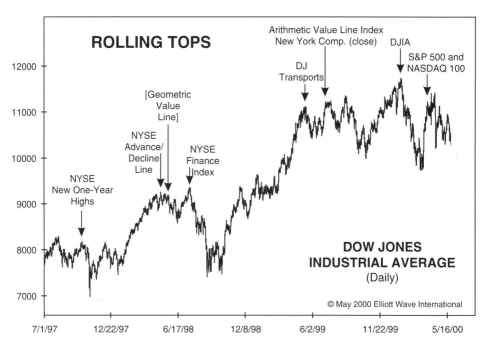

© May 2000 Elliott Wave International

below), setting off long term sentiment alarms like never before. Most stocks have already been going down so long that many believe the bear market must be *over*. In fact, it has only begun. By simply lasting a long time, the top has produced one of its all-time great foolers. As we have noted before, its long duration confirms the Grand Supercycle dimension of the peak. The last holdout is the Dow Jones Utility Average, which is consistent with our call for "one final new all-time high" in the February issue. The utilities registered a new high in May and could go higher in coming days. This would be a poignant wave good-bye to the Grand Supercycle bull market, as the Utility Average was the last major average to peak in 1929.

[Note: The NYSE Utilities had peaked two months before, and the Dow Utilities peaked six months later. — Ed.]

Valuation

Stock market valuation in March 2000 will probably stand as the outer limit for centuries. Notice the bullets marking the S&P 400's valuation in September 1929 and July 1932. These show what happens when the gravitational pull of normalcy reasserts itself after a historic *over*valuation. The trip back always takes investor psychology past average valuations to at least the low end of the normal range shown by the box in this chart (next page), now dwarfed in size by the utterly outrageous extremes attending the stock mania of the 1990s. Now that tech stocks are in retreat, one of the popular things to say is that the "rationale for the boom" got out of hand, and the decline marks a return to common sense. This sudden onset of sanity has reputedly produced the rebirth of the "old economy" and thus, relative strength for the Dow. The mantra is, "valuation matters again." If history is any guide, the bulls had better hope this is false.

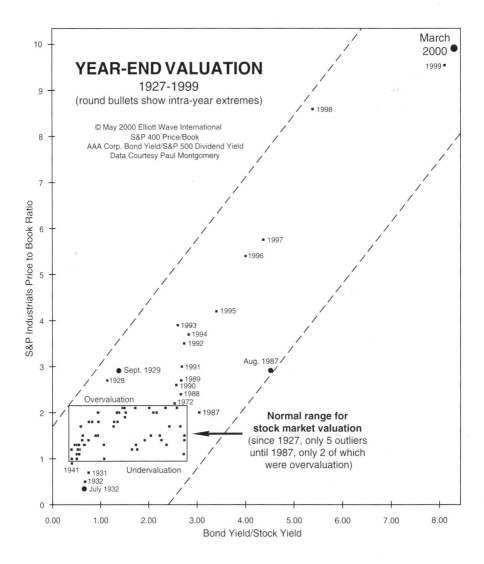

YEAR-END VALUATION

1927-1999

(round bullets show intra-year extremes)

© May 2000 Elliott Wave International
S&P 400 Price/Book
AAA Corp. Bond Yield/S&P 500 Dividend Yield
Data Courtesy Paul Montgomery

S&P Industrials Price to Book Ratio

March 2000
1999
1998
1997
1996
1995
1993
1994
1992
Sept. 1929
1928
1991
1989
1990
1988
1972
Aug. 1987
Overvaluation
1987
Normal range for
stock market valuation
(since 1927, only 5 outliers
until 1987, only 2 of which
were overvaluation)
1941
1931
1932
July 1932
Undervaluation

Bond Yield/Stock Yield

July 2000

Rationalizing High Stock Valuation

Most analysts who justify the present historically high valuations for stocks cite "a strong economy" and "low inflation" as excuses. A brief review of history shows that in precisely such environments, P/E, P/D, P/book and bond/stock yield ratios can be very high (such as now) or very low (such as in the 1940s), so there is no reliable linear correlation between these two conditions and stock valuations. That evidence summarily invalidates the argument.

Yet there is more to say. The celebrated "low inflation" during the 1980s-1990s bull market is partly a chimera because inflation has in fact been roaring throughout the past 20 years, particularly in the realm of credit expansion, which has fueled the gains primarily in stock and real estate prices as opposed to good prices.

The greatest error of those who justify current stock valuations, though, is in attaching, for example, the P/E ratio to conclusions about absolute stock prices. Even if one were to argue that today's high P/E ratios are justified, he would not therefore have a basis upon which to defend the current level of stock prices. As 1929-1932 revealed, prices can fall 90% even as the P/E ratio maintains. You cannot own the P/E ratio; you can own only stocks, and that's where you can lose your shirt if you listen to arguments based upon the premise of linear event causality, which are improper for, and inapplicable to, financial forecasting. Every such approach to market forecasting is doomed from the start by being based upon false premises. To understand how markets work, you have to understand how people think. Again, this does not mean that those who have such an understanding will always be right. It does mean, however, that those who do not are flying blind and leading you to take unwarranted risk.

July 23, 2000

"All We Need..."

Author Unknown

To: Robert R. Prechter
Sent: Sunday July 23, 2000 10:30 a.m.
Subject: Bob: I found this on the web.

The fact that I am favoring a continuation of the boom rather than a collapse may be a sign of "contagion." Here is an email I just sent: I have heard P.Q. Wall expound on how the 1929 top unfolded— I will be watching the numbers you mentioned closely—One thing of many things that always repeat is, at the end of the generational move, virtually NO ONE knows it's ending until long after the fact—I always monitor my own psychology— a self-conscious monitoring — lately, I have been favoring Wolanchuk's thesis of an endless boom....yet fully realising that my view would be perfectly typical of a long-term skeptic finally throwing in the towel and joining the bulls — in other words, I have become a great contrary indicator — Two people, I think, lend credence to the case that an end is near rather than a continuation. The author, in 1990, of [one of the most bearish books of the last 20 years] is now wildly bullish and a believer that something "is different" this time — he has been, like so many others, worn down by the sheer persistence of this mega-bull market — now all we need for the final proof is Robert Prechter to become bullish on stocks.

A Major Stock Market Low is Still Due in 2003-2004

The Elliott Wave Theorist's cyclic and Fibonacci projections have long pointed to the year 2003 (with leeway to 2004) for a major low in the stock market. This low should mark Supercycle wave (a) of Grand Supercycle wave Ⓘ. This bottom is expected to be of the magnitude of those registered in 1932, 1842, 1784 (±8) and 1722.

Several previous years have appeared to be good candidates for the bull market top, but none of them panned out. At this point, time is running out, and if our low is to occur on schedule, very little guesswork remains. This report will present a review of my cycle and Fibonacci studies to bring you up to date on the dramatic potential that lies directly ahead.

Kondratieff Cycle

In the early 1980s, there was serious debate about the timing of the previous Kondratieff cycle low. Was it 1932 or 1942? Today, of course, no one believes that the Kondratieff cycle exists, as they are convinced that economic cycles have been tamed by the Federal Reserve Board, and the trend is always up.

In May 1983, *The Elliott Wave Theorist* looked at the history of that cycle and the evidence of stock market action and concluded as follows: "Based on its previous low in 1896, the most recent Kondratieff cycle bottom…may have occurred as late as 1949, which places the next bottom around **2003**." Ever since EWT came to that conclusion, additional evidence has strengthened the case.

Should we rely on the Kondratieff cycle? Here is how *At the Crest of the Tidal Wave* answered that question:

> Most economists dismiss cycles altogether and appear particularly to relish denying the existence of the Kondratieff cycle. I take a strong position on the opposite side. While the time length for the Kondratieff cycle is usually cited as "50 to 60 years, averaging about 54 years in length," the record of stock prices reveals that this cycle has recently

been quite precise. As you can see by [the Figure below], price lows occurred in 1896, **53** years before 1949, and in 1842, **54** years before 1896, and (possibly) 1788, **54** years before 1842. Sparse data indicates that the latter date could have been any of several years between 1778 and 1788 (see discussion in Chapter 2 [of *At the Crest of the Tidal Wave*]). The cycle that occurred in the 1700s in British stock prices appears to have been longer, at **62** years, lasting from 1722 to 1784. The answer, then, is that if the cycle is still operating, our timing projection should be fairly reliable. The earliest likely year for a bottom is **2002**, the best fit is **2003**, and a match of the longest cycle on record would place the low as far out as **2011**.

Figure 1 displays the history of the Kondratieff cycle against the Dow Jones Industrial Average. Figure 2 shows a close-up of the last two cycles against the PPI-adjusted DJIA, revealing why I dated the cycle bottom later than other cycle-watchers. The 1929 high and subsequent crash occurred early in the down portion of the cycle, which is why Kondratieff cycle enthusiasts were thrown off about the position of the previous cycle bottom. Inflation-adjusted stock prices scraped bottom until the cycle finally ceased exerting downside pressure. For the record, 1948 was the end of the cycle in PPI-adjusted terms, while 1949 was the end of the cycle in nominal terms, so the proper designation for the low is 1948-1949.

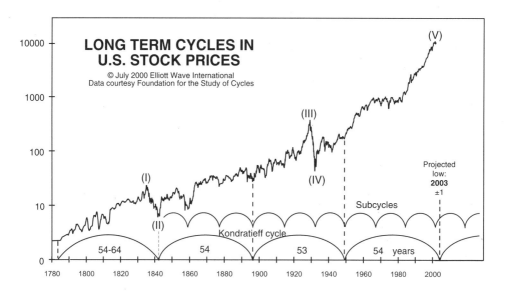

Figure 1

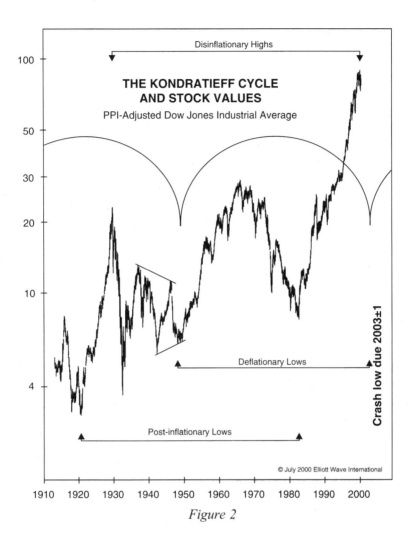

Figure 2

   With all-time highs being achieved this year (in fact, two indexes are at an all-time high as this is written), most people would think that the idea of a major stock market low three years from now is absurd. In fact, though, three of the last four Kondratieff-related stock market bottoms occurred within a few short years of an all-time high stock market peak: 1720-1722: *2 years*; 1835-1842: *7 years*; 1929-1932: *3 years*. In two of the four cases (1722 and 1835), the stock market topped extremely late in the Kondratieff cycle and then crashed. This is the prospect we face today.

The Benner-Fibonacci Cycle

A.J. Frost worked out a pattern of cyclic repetition that has a basis in the Fibonacci sequence. We presented the idea in Chapter 4 of *Elliott Wave Principle* in 1978. In that book, we showed the progression of the cycles through 1987, which we forecast as the next important low. *At the Crest of the Tidal Wave* presented the extended progression, calling for the next low in 2003, coincident with the projected Kondratieff cycle low. Figure 3 shows the entire Benner-Fibonacci cycle chart from 1895 through 2003.

At least as interesting as the next projected bottom is the fact that Benner-Fibonacci cycles also project a *top* in the year 2000, i.e., *now*. For the record, note that the 1896 low occurred eight months after the projected bottom of 1895, and the 1974 and 1994 lows occurred one month prior to the projected bottoms of 1975 and 1995. No cyclic model is perfect, but these projections have nevertheless been quite a good guide.

Fibonacci Durations

Figure 4 shows the Fibonacci web of peaks that began in 1966. From there to the top in 1987 took **21** years. Had the current Kondratieff cycle acted like the previous one, that year would have been the high in stock prices. However, following the crash, the market resumed its upward path and has now climbed an additional **13** years, for a total of **34** years from the 1966 high. Thus, two Fibonacci durations related to tops end in 2000. As you can see in Figure 5, this feat has produced a secondary Fibonacci result, which is that wave V from 1974 now subdivides into two phases of advance lasting a Fibonacci **13** years each.

Figure 6 shows that a remarkable four Fibonacci durations related to stock market bottoms all end in 2003. That year is **13** years from 1990, when the three-year bear market in the Value Line index ended, completing the largest setback within the two-decade stock mania. It is **21** years from 1982, the bottom of the 16-year bear market in the inflation-adjusted Dow. It is **55** years from 1948, the end of the 19-year bear-market triangle in the inflation-adjusted DJIA. It is **144** years from 1859, the end of Supercycle wave (II). This is a remarkable cluster of dates all pointing to the same year.

Together, these clusters project a major high in the year **2000** and a major low in the year **2003**. Notice that these Fibonacci durations, while unrelated to the Benner-Fibonacci cycles and the Kondratieff cycle, *nevertheless indicate the same years for a major top and bottom.*

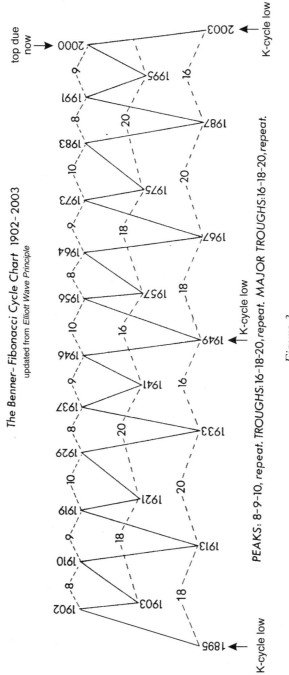

The Benner-Fibonacci Cycle Chart 1902-2003
updated from *Elliott Wave Principle*

top due now → 2000

2003 ← K-cycle low

1995
1991
6
1987
16
1983
8
20
1975
10
1973
20
1967
6
1964
18
1957
8
18
1956
K-cycle low
10
16
1949 ←
1946
6
1941
16
1937
8
1933
1929
20
10
1921
20
1919
18
1913
6
1910
18
8
1903
1902
1895 ← K-cycle low

PEAKS: 8-9-10, repeat. TROUGHS:16-18-20,repeat. MAJOR TROUGHS:16-18-20,repeat.

Figure 3

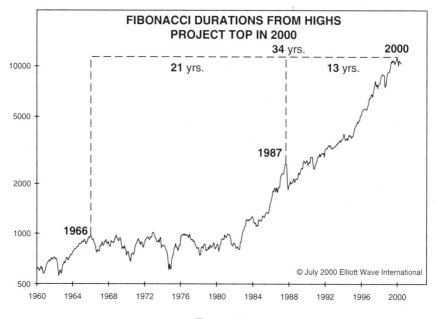

Figure 4

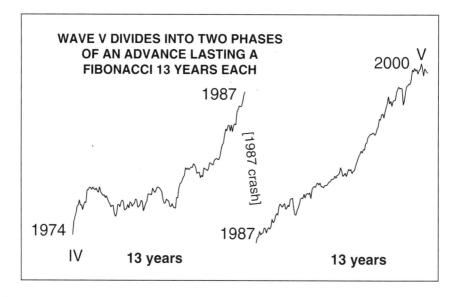

Figure 5

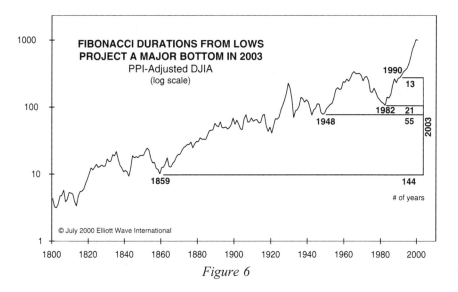

FIBONACCI DURATIONS FROM LOWS
PROJECT A MAJOR BOTTOM IN 2003
PPI-Adjusted DJIA
(log scale)

Figure 6

The 3-Year Cycle

Back in 1978, I predicted in *Elliott Wave Principle* that the 4-year cycle would shrink to 3.5 years because a whole new Elliott wave of Cycle degree was due to begin. The cycle shrank immediately thereafter, averaging 3.3 years in length, with bottoms in 1978, 1981, 1984, 1987, 1990, 1994 (January) and 1997. The next two bottoms are due at **year-end 2000**, ±2 months and in the first half of **2004**. See Figure 7.

Only One Year's Leeway

Several considerations suggest that the low could occur as late as 2004, which is a small allowance given the substantial length of the Kondratieff cycle. The 3.25-year cycle is ideally due to bottom in early 2004, as detailed above. The Decennial Pattern is an average of the market's action each decade. The fact that the pattern produces an Elliott wave (see discussion in *Elliott Wave Principle*) adds to its validity. It would be nothing more than a statistical artifact were it not for the fact that the market has tended to follow the pattern in each individual decade. The pattern bottoms in the second year of the decade, with little upside progress until the middle of the fourth year. In two recent decades, the zero and fourth years, rather than the second year, have marked lows: 1970/1974 and 1990/1994. It could

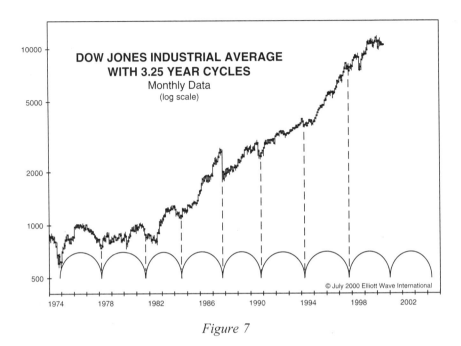

Figure 7

happen again. Alternatively, recall that the market tested its 1932 low in 1933 with an 80% retracement of the first wave up. If 2003 marks the bottom, 2004 could include a deep setback to test that low. As you can see in Figure 8, downside pressure from the Decennial pattern ends just shy of midway through the "4" year. The economy typically lags the stock market, so if stocks collapse into 2003, the severest year of the resulting depression should be 2004, so *some* measures will probably bottom then. Finally, because the preceding Kondratieff cycle lasted only 53 years to 1949 (or 52 years to 1948), the current cycle might stretch to 2004 to maintain the 54-year average.

The 20-year cycle bottoms in 2002, as you can see in Figure 9. There seems to be too little time for the stock market to bottom that quickly, but the 1720-1722 experience (see discussion below) shows that it is possible. My guess is that the pressure from this cycle will simply make the year leading up to its low the most powerful portion of the decline.

Probable Depth and Results

Kondratieff-cycle stock-market collapses of the past three centuries have ranged from 46% to 98%. In 1720-1722, the average stock on the

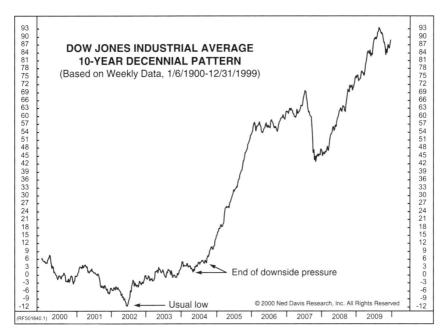

Figure 8

Figure 9

London exchange, properly factoring in those that dropped to zero, fell 98%. The decline that ended in 1784 is difficult to assess, as the crash of 1720-1722 dampened stock speculation for a century. The depression of the early 1790s was severe, covering the Americas and Europe, so regardless of the exact figures, it was clearly a disaster for whatever stock owners there were. In 1835-1842, a reconstructed average of U.S. stocks fell 78%. The smallest decline, which occurred from 1889 to 1896, was not preceded by excessive stock speculation. Moreover, it took place within the middle of a strongly advancing third Elliott wave that lasted from 1859 to 1929. It is remarkable that in the middle of this most powerful structure, and without stocks reaching absurd heights beforehand, the Kondratieff cycle still managed to cut an average of major stock prices in half. In 1929-1932, the Dow fell 89%. Even this substantial figure does not take into account the many company names that were flying high in 1928 but no longer existed in 1933. Figure 10 summarizes these declines. *The decline that lies immediately ahead will be in the range of these percentages.*

The last time a Grand Supercycle peaked out was in 1720. Thus, the only decline among the past four Kondratieff-cycle collapses that coincided with the kickoff of a Grand Supercycle bear market was 1720-1722,

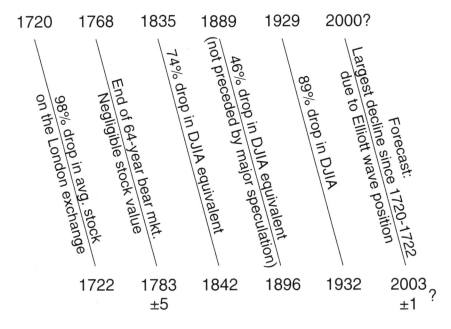

Figure 10

the 98% wipe-out. *That is the degree of wave ending today.* The extent of the 1990s stock mania, with its legions of pricey shares of companies having no actual worth, brings us to a year that resembles none more than 1720, which ended the South Sea Bubble in England. The situation today is certainly set up to produce a similar result, as shares valued in the billions of dollars today are often of companies that not only have no earnings but also persistently lose money. The number of stocks poised to go to zero is so large that the coming bear market should have little difficulty producing an experience more akin to that of 1720-1722 than to any Kondratieff cycle decline since. Figure 5-12 in *At the Crest of the Tidal Wave* presents a full picture of the forecasted Grand Supercycle as I see it.

Each Supercycle collapse and every Kondratieff cycle bottom has produced a depression in the economy. A severe depression took place in the 1720s, 1790s, 1840s, 1896-1897 and the 1930s. There is little question that the upcoming decline will have the same result.

For most people, cash will be a good friend during the coming stock price fall. However, today's market is unique in that it offers so many ways to profit from falling prices, whether via special "bear" funds, liquid derivatives or short-side portfolio management. To the speculator properly positioned, the next three to four years should offer the most profit potential in the shortest amount of time in the history of the stock market.

The Elliott Wave Financial Forecast

July 28, 2000

"New Economy" Fever

In February's Special Report on "Deflation and The New Economy," *The Elliott Wave Financial Forecast* showed the rapid rise in media references to the "New Economy" and noted that the "more exaggerated and insistent the reports of the triumph of the New Economy become, the more emphatically they reveal the hidden fact that the economy is back where it was in the fall of 1929, at the cusp of a great deflationary downturn." In the first half of 2000, the rate of New Economy stories surged again, this time by a factor of 10. Even as the NASDAQ collapsed and "dot-com companies offering crazy bargains to win customers" spread to big suppliers like Sun Microsystems and Hewlett-Packard, the threat of deflation through asset devaluation has gone almost completely unrecognized.

The Atlanta Journal-Constitution
Bill Shipp's Georgia

August 21, 2000

Bust Just Ahead?
Bob Prechter's Bear Watch Project

by Doug Monroe
Special to Bill Shipp's Georgia

Robert Prechter is one scary guy.

Prechter is the reclusive stock market and social trend predictor who lives by Lake Lanier and crops up in the news every now and then with cool descriptions of economic apocalypse.

I've seen articles mentioning him and his people recently in *Georgia Trend* and the *Atlanta Business Chronicle*.

I guess that means the boy is back!

Prechter is a youthful-looking, guitar-picking Yalie who has been around for years and, for a while, was hugely famous because he correctly predicted the current bull market in stocks in a 1978 book.

Then he predicted the 1987 crash, although some sourpusses quibble about his timing. I've followed him on his Web site (www.elliottwave.com) for years.

When he predicted the bull market, he also predicted it would end in a cataclysmic bear market. But the bull has run far longer than Prechter thought it would.

A while back I sent Prechter and his folks a copy of a book by my favorite obscure dead psychoanalyst, Dr. Edmund Bergler, who believed humans are driven by an unconscious desire to suffer.

Bergler's theory explains a lot about Atlanta traffic, among other things.

If Bergler was right, our unconscious desire to suffer would lead us to invest our money in places where we will lose it painfully. This is why gamblers gamble — not because of the burning desire to win, but because of the deeper unconscious desire to lose.

Bergler can be scarier than Prechter!

Prechter studies the Elliott wave theory that human behavior moves in cycles that can be tracked and even predicted. The stock market is so numbers-oriented that it's one of the best ways to work the theory.

Most serious stockbrokers and analysts dismissed Prechter years ago. A lot of them think Federal Reserve Board Chairman Alan Greenspan has healed economic cycles, like an evangelist, and the stock market will only go up over time.

But Prechter's not the only person talking about the footsteps of a big scary bear.

Yale economist Robert J. Schiller has written a hot-selling book, *Irrational Exuberance*, in which he says a psychological herd effect, not smart investing, has driven today's stock prices to sky-high levels.

Prechter has been writing about the psychological herd effect for years.

So, if he's right, what will happen?

Back in 1983, Prechter's newsletter, *The Elliott Wave Theorist*, placed the next stock market bottom around the year 2003. That's his story and he's sticking to it.

That bottom will not be like the crash in 1929 that preceded the Great Depression and saw an 89-percent drop in the Dow Jones Industrial Average by 1932, Prechter says.

It will be more like the end of the South Sea Bubble, 1720-1722, which saw a 98 percent drop in the average stock on the London exchange, he predicts. A large number of today's stocks are poised to go to zero, he adds.

That kind of drop could make some 401(k)s look mighty puny at retirement time.

We've built a dream world around the bull market, investing billions of dollars in companies that don't make money.

Our herd behavior is putting us into stretch limos and huge SUVs and fake stucco McMansions, while the media throws confetti.

An entire generation of young people has entered the job market since the crash of 1987 and knows no direction but up.

Yet some of them are tasting defeat for the first time as they pick up pink slips from failing dot-com companies.

I think some members of the herd can feel the big one coming, like little forest animals before an earthquake.

Some of us may secretly suspect that something awful could happen to something as magical and mighty as our economy, but we're in denial, at least on the conscious level.

That's why so many of us went to see *Titanic*, which was a terrible movie but a powerful psychic symbol.

The vision of the unsinkable ocean liner going to the bottom of the sea struck a chord in a lot of souls, for reasons we couldn't figure out.

It was terrifying, yet millions of us stood in line to see it. That's why I subscribe to Prechter's newsletter and visit his Web site.

Horror is such good, clean fun.

October 27, 2000

GE 1974-2000 = phi x 100

by Peter Kendall, Elliott Wave International

General Electric was one of the last stocks to complete its bull market with a final high on August 28. As late as October 5, GE, the only original member of the Dow Jones Industrial Average, was within a fraction of its all-time peak. Subscriber Alvery Bartlett points out that GE expanded from a September 1974 low of 0.625 to 60.5. As the chart shows, GE advanced to nearly 100 times the Fibonacci ratio in a fine-looking Elliott-wave pattern that began a few months before the overall bull market and finished a few months after its completion. While we are not about to say that GE can't try to make it up to 62.5 just to make it perfect, the long-term picture is what counts. While the Dow achieved a 20x multiple from the 1974 low, GE achieved a 100x multiple, *five times as much.* In the process, the company switched a good part of its focus from manufacturing to finance. (Its holdings and thus its bubble-era valuation include CNBC.) When the markets collapse, so will the finance business. GE's consumer products aren't nearly as good as they were during wave III (1942-1966). We want to be the first to say it out loud: GE is going to go *way* down over the next four years.

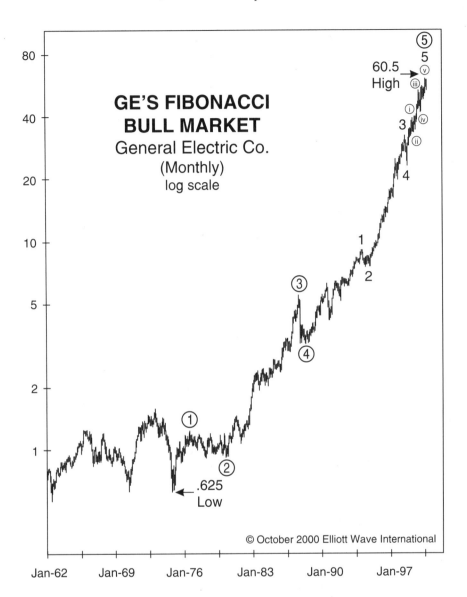

**GE'S FIBONACCI
BULL MARKET**
General Electric Co.
(Monthly)
log scale

60.5
High

.625
Low

© October 2000 Elliott Wave International

Jan-62   Jan-69   Jan-76   Jan-83   Jan-90   Jan-97

December 1, 2000

The Economy

by Peter Kendall

Guess which of these economic assessments is from the November 21, 2000 issue of *The Wall Street Journal*:

Feast Will Go On

An array of new forecasts predict a rosy future for the nation's economy. Analysts raised their forecasts for the next year. "This is not an economy that's about to take a plunge."

A Gloomy Vocabulary Describes the Scene

One word used by economists to describe the current business outlook is "bleak." Another is "grim." But whichever words business analysts use to characterize the current scene, they are all negative; there are few optimists around these days. And with good cause.

Readers of our book, *The Wave Principle of Human Social Behavior*, know the answer to this one. Obviously, the first outlook is the most recent. The second is from *Business Week* at the December 1974 bottom for stocks. We should hear the same pessimism from the economic experts at the next low in 2003 or 2004, *after* the low in stock prices. The forecast of a "rosy future" is actually more bearish than *Business Week*'s 1974 gloom was bullish because it comes after the prices of many of the most sensitive measures of *future* economic performance, like semiconductors, copper, lumber, scrap steel and stocks themselves, have fallen by big amounts. Last month, we showed another leading economic indicator, the Junk Bond Index, breaking through its low at the 1990 recession. That break has since been followed by a further decline of 8.8%, as the media issued renewed calls for "a huge rally" in the sector. This faith in a highly speculative "investment" that sits on its all-time low does not bode well for junk bonds or the economy. Together with reports of the slowest growth in four years in the third quarter, it suggests strongly that further tangible evidence of not a soft landing, but a *crash* landing, is dead ahead.

Section Two
RETROSPECTIVE:
ERRORS MADE AND
KNOWLEDGE GAINED

Perspective

The Real Bull Market

How you view the timing of *At the Crest of the Tidal Wave*'s bearish message to the public and *The Elliott Wave Theorist*'s staunch stance thereafter depends on what you know about the bull market. Most people date the bull market from 1982 and say that it ended in the first quarter of 2000. That's accurate enough for the Dow, but the true bull market unequivocally began in the fourth quarter of 1974. After having been bearish the overall stock market since 1972, I turned to long term bullish in early January, 1975, when for the first time I bought a list of common stocks.

Take a look at Figure 1, which reflects percentage gains in the average stock, and you will see how clearly December 1974 marked the lift-off of the great bull market. In fact, the average stock was soaring through the latter half of the 1970s as the Dow languished. While the Dow's lagging action was frustrating for forecasting purposes, *being long term bullish throughout that period was the correct stance*. Between the 1974 low and the 1982 low, the average stock tripled. When the Dow finally took off in 1982, it was only playing catch-up.

Saying "SELL" on October 5, 1987 was a great call, as it avoided the 1987 crash and over three years of net losses in stocks. There was nothing wrong with getting aggressively bearish in 1989, either. From there, the Dow Jones Transports collapsed 50 percent, the Value Line index plummeted nearly to match its 1987 low, and in 1990-1991, the economy went into recession. The Japanese market topped out for good on the last day of 1989 and never looked back.

The stock market recovery after 1990 was so sluggish that it barely caught up with the return from Treasury bills from the 1987 high through 1994. From 1995 through 1999, though, was entirely another matter, as blue chips and "momentum" stocks, caught in a mania, outpaced every other investment. I was not along for the ride.

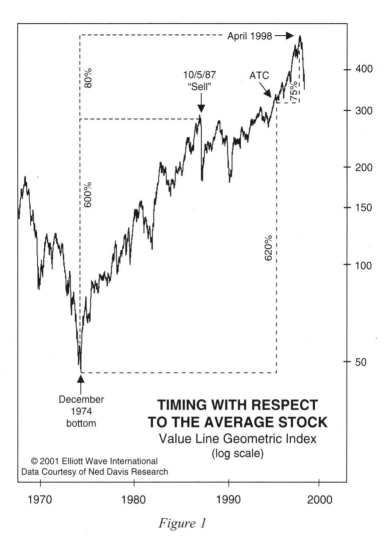

Figure 1

I released *At the Crest* in mid-1995, 21 long years after the bull market began and after a 620 percent gain in the average stock. It was less than three years from the top in the Value Line index, which gained only another 75 percent and then retraced nearly all of it in mid-1998 in a few short months! On the other hand, the popular averages rose nearly five additional years and significantly compounded previous gains. The Dow, which had gone up 8 times since 1974, went up another 2½ times from there. So if you were an investor in the average stock, you had one outcome; if you were a blue chip or "index" investor, you had another. Being five years off is not much in the context of identifying the end of a 216-year Grand Supercycle wave (think of being five *days* early out of 216). It is nevertheless a lot to miss when you're living through it, particularly when your guide is mis-reading all the signposts.

Big Mistakes

My timing errors for the major averages during this period were legion. I called way too many tops and was wrong time after time, which became embarrassing. In some cases, it was because wave V had reached or exceeded the upper boundary of its channel. In others, my conviction was due to long-term Fibonacci relationships in prices and duration that I thought would end the advance. Corrections were shallow and upwardly skewed, so waves were difficult to read. Several times, upside momentum waned, as at a top, and then uncharacteristically accelerated. Professionals and the public were historically bullish, which is normally the condition right at a top, yet the market ploughed upward as if benefitting from an endless supply of rocket fuel. Idiots appeared to be savants. People with no background in market analysis — from media pundits to barbers to basket-ball players — would call for more rise, and up the market would go. For the first time since 1927-1929, the lemmings ran on with total abandon, and the cliff refused to appear. The stampede had to meet its end, and end it surely has, though not without making veteran market analysts look fool-ish. Being a leader of that pack was hardly an honor.

An Elliottician, if he is widely followed, can anticipate his own peri-ods of error. For example, as you read earlier in this book, the March 18, 1987 issue of *The Wall Street Journal* quoted me as follows:

> "I'm probably going to be wrong about something in a big way around the top.... I'll probably express caution too early, in which case people will say baloney on this crash stuff."

I expanded on that comment a few months later in *USA Today*'s October 9, 1987 issue, which was four days after one of the best calls I ever made. Because of my own professional wave pattern, I knew that those good for-tunes and the way people viewed my persona were about to change:

> Although he's now riding high, he has no illusions that it will last for-ever. Like the stock market travels along those waves he and Ralph Nelson Elliott made famous, Prechter knows there are some dips in store... "There will come a time that people will focus on the bad calls."

The social imperative required that I be generally disbelieved at a major turn, and the only way I could imagine that situation occurring was to presume that I would make errors and the media would trash my image by focusing on my bad calls. These developments would then allow the majority of investors to ignore my warnings just when they mattered most. The irony of such a prediction, though, is that despite your knowledge, you cannot change the outcome.

Calling Too Many Tops

Being resolutely bearish in the face of immense public and professional pressure to capitulate was a challenge. That position, I believe, will ultimately be vindicated, but it also has had a big downside: calling too many tops. The next few pages graphically depict the erroneous "top" forecasts made in *The Elliott Wave Theorist* after the Dow moved past the upside target of 3686/3885 initially projected in the September 1982 issue (reprinted in the Appendix to *Elliott Wave Principle*). I am sparing you the accompanying prose, but you will find the dates on the charts. In the middle, you will find some commentary from late 1996, when I recognized that the Cycle degree trendchannel was governing the advance. As you will see thereafter, that's when I began to get my perspective back. Even so, the final high was a long time coming. After this, we will get to our belated reward: new information about how Elliott waves behave, which starts on page 164.

Focusing On The Wrong Degree

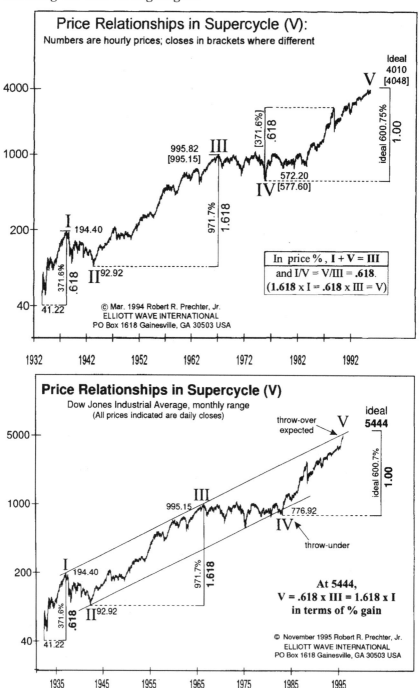

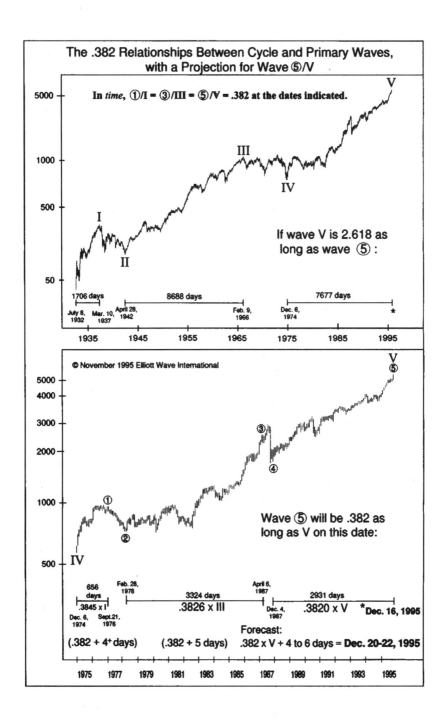

The .382 Relationships Between Cycle and Primary Waves, with a Projection for Wave ⑤/V

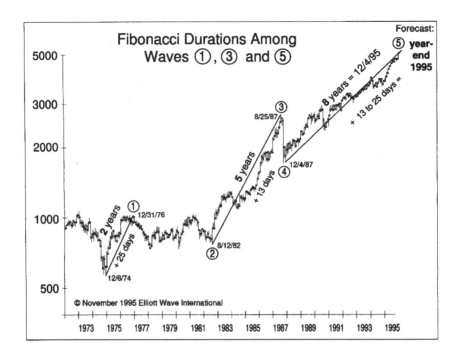

"The entire infrastructure of the nation collapsed today, rapidly
followed by the Dow rising through 5000 for the first time."

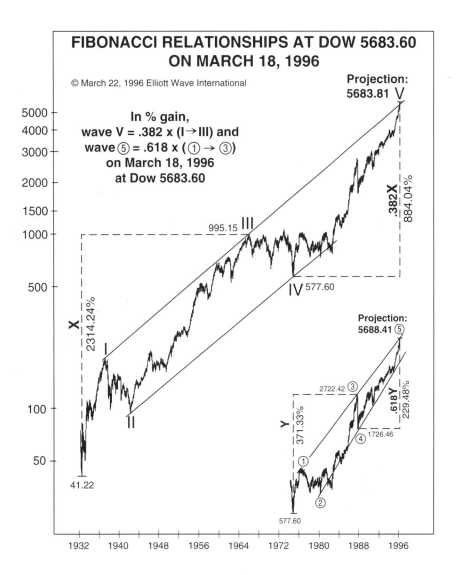

FIBONACCI RELATIONSHIPS AT DOW 5683.60
ON MARCH 18, 1996

© March 22, 1996 Elliott Wave International

In % gain,
wave V = .382 x (I→III) and
wave ⑤ = .618 x (① → ③)
on March 18, 1996
at Dow 5683.60

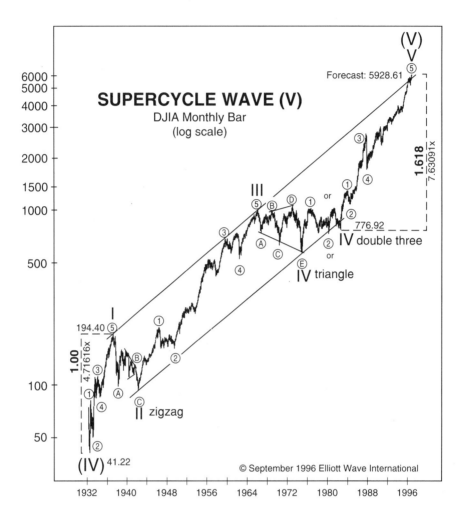

SUPERCYCLE WAVE (V)
DJIA Monthly Bar
(log scale)

Forecast: 5928.61

III

IV double three

IV triangle

II zigzag

(IV) 41.22

© September 1996 Elliott Wave International

The Elliott Wave Theorist

November 26/December 6, 1996

When a market
(1) ignores its historical range of valuation,
(2) decelerates without reversing, then re-accelerates, continually,
(3) surpasses long-standing resistance lines,
(4) creates no reactions, only pauses, and
(5) continues relentlessly in a direction fully anticipated by the majority, it is usually in a blowoff.

In such an environment, near-to-intermediate term waves, cycles and momentum indicators are useless because there are virtually no waves or cycles of which to take advantage. In the current case, the only wave that is relevant is the one at Grand Supercycle degree, a rare historical trend culmination that is bulldozing every other degree out of its path. Since history is what market analysts use as a guide, anything unprecedented in the available data makes for a difficult and painful time, and that's what we are having.

When tracking *commodity* bull markets, blowoffs are to be expected. Those advances are the product of fear (of shortage), and that emotion culminates in panic, which ends at its extreme point. Stock bull markets, by contrast, almost always end with *deceleration*, providing "sell signals" in momentum indicators and often producing tops that are rounded. The reason is that mass ebullience does not culminate at its extreme point but dissipates slowly. The U.S. stock market has always topped out along the lines of the ebullience model. It has not accelerated into a top in the history of the country. There are hints that we may be facing an exception.

It is common for triangles in the stock market to be followed by thrusts (see text, p.52), which are short fifth waves. The five-month-long triangle that *The Elliott Wave Theorist* identified the day after it bottomed in July was clear enough, and we called for a sharp rally to end not much beyond the May high. The market averages initially followed the script, even to the point of slowing their ascent in September-October. Instead of topping, it has suddenly accelerated (in speed, at least, though not in breadth), exceeding all resistance lines. The picture has begun to look much more like what we often see in commodities. Triangles in commodities typically precede *extended* fifth waves, which carry to dizzy heights and end in a blowoff. If this were a commodity, we might have expected a huge rise with upside acceleration. But it's not a commodity; it's the stock market.

Or is it? At least once in history, stocks served as a focal point for a commodity-like mania: in 1720, when the South Sea Bubble hypnotized all of England. Its aftermath was a 98% drop in the value of the average stock in two years. The top was a near-vertical spike, just as we see so often in long term charts of commodities. The most dramatic example of such behavior that I observed first-hand was silver in 1978-1980. It, too, emerged from a triangle correction, at about $4 an ounce. Its fifth wave was of reasonable length at $9. It hit a long term resistance line on semilog scale just above $18, meeting *The Elliott Wave Theorist's* forecast for the top. Bursting through that line, it then tacked on a 2.618 multiple of *that* price in less than two months, reaching $50. After that, it crashed back to $11, a 78% drop, in eight weeks.

Has the psychology behind the invention of stock index futures commoditized the behavior of the stock indexes themselves? EWT commented last April that this bull market in stocks did not appear to be built upon prosperity and ebullience but on desperation. People know Social Security is bankrupt; they know Medicare is going broke. The economy is growing at a snail's pace, and their productive effort is substantially wiped out by taxes and regulation. They rightfully fear that if they rely only on their salaries and businesses, their kids won't go to college, and they won't have anything saved for retirement. So they borrow and speculate to make up the difference. That observation suggests a correlation between the psychology behind this stock market and that of a commodity bull market. This is not a big party thrown to celebrate good times; it is a big capitulation born of desperate times.

If the stock market is to end its upside performance as a commodity would, the end will come on an intraday spike top on huge volume, the reverse image of a stock market crash low. If a semblance of "stockness" remains, there will ultimately be a pullback, then a slower rally, indicating deceleration. This second case might be difficult to identify immediately, as the bull market has already slowed countless times since 1991 only to re-accelerate in a way unprecedented in this century except for the experience of 1927-1928. If the market does decelerate once again while rising, we will be certain that the trend has changed only when we see *persistence* in the opposite direction. Just a couple of weeks of steady daily declines, such as occurred off the top in 1929 and after the high in Japanese stocks at the end of 1989, will be enough to say that the bubble has burst.

Most of the time, a thorough knowledge of a subject pays off. In the realm of mass market psychology, there are times when those *least* knowledgeable appear as geniuses and roll in ledger-entry money. Today, I almost wish we had been among those people, but they have two problems. First, did you know that *Investor's Daily*'s mutual fund average is still below its May high? It's true; only the blue chips have soared in this move, and few have been smart enough to be in them exclusively. Second, when the tide turns, their stress and disappointment will be worse than what we are going through now, if you can imagine that. Here on the left side of the top, knowing that we will avoid their fate seems a negligible comfort. On the right side of the turn, we will feel very different, I can assure you. In the meantime, avoid exposure to the stock market except for long term puts (leaps), where loss is limited and potential gain from a 1997 crash remains high.

We are not without a handle on the possibilities. While the Dow has exceeded its Supercycle trend channel, a parallel channel at Cycle degree, which formerly looked like a ridiculous construct, provides a picture of upside potential. This approach was the only tool that worked in marking the end of the explosive final move in gold at the end of the 1970s and in stocks at the end of the 1920s. If the Dow reaches the parallel line depicted here at Cycle degree, we will be able to recognize the event.

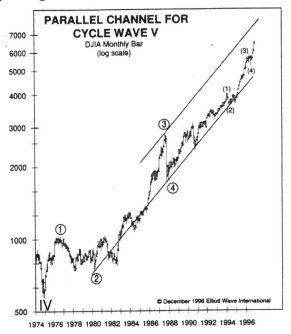

Still Early But Gaining Perspective

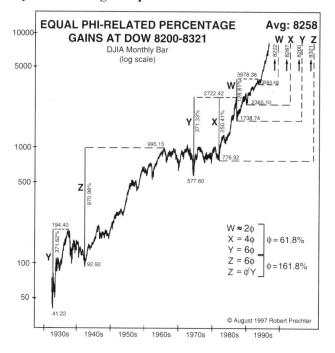

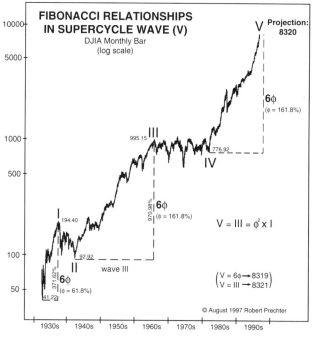

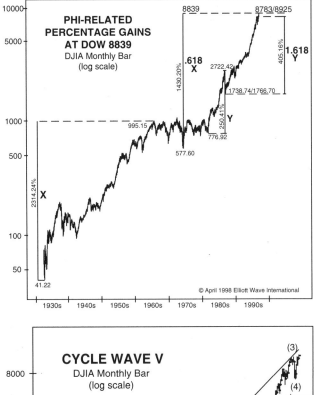

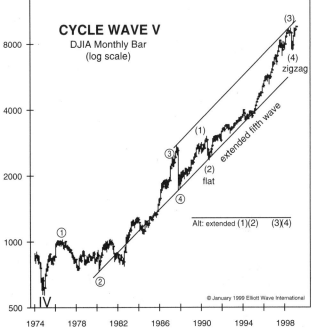

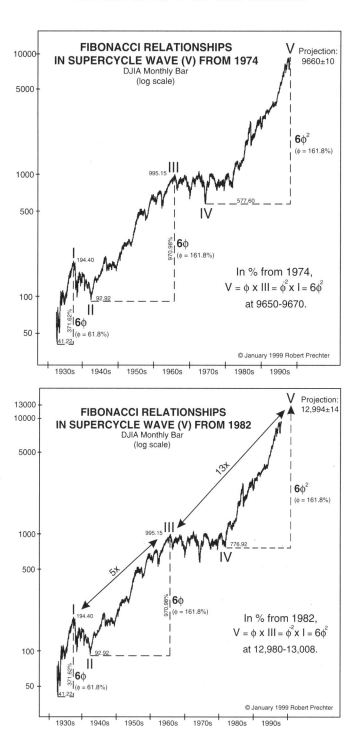

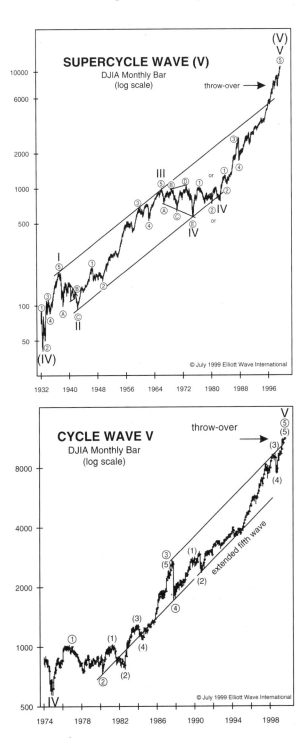

The Elliott Wave Financial Forecast

December 3, 1999

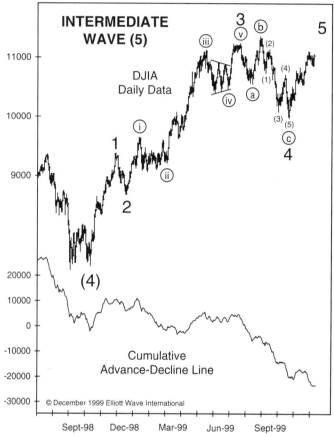

This week's action, culminating with the Dow's explosive rise on December 3, confirms the alternate count discussed in the last two issues. In October, we noted that the five-wave decline from the all-time high could also mark the completion of "an expanded flat for Minor wave 4 or possibly 2." The chart above labels the five-wave decline from the all-time high as wave ⓒ of an expanded flat correction for Minor wave 4. Given this labeling, a logical target for the rally is 11,889, where wave 5 will equal wave 1. In the May 1998 issue, subscriber Steve Rock noted, "The next Fibonacci price relationship where the percentage gain of wave V from 1982 will be .618 of wave I through III, gives a target of 11,889," so we now have an additional reason to focus on that level. However, given the depth of wave 4, wave 5 could fall short of normal targets.

The Elliott Wave Financial Forecast
Interim Report

February 22, 2000

The DJIA's break of 10,355 confirms that a bear trend started at the 11,750 [intraday] high of January 14. The 11% decline in the first seven weeks of the year is the Dow's worst comparable start to a new year since 1920, which at the time saw the index in the midst of a bear market that dropped the average 48% from October 1919 to August 1921. All three Dow averages appear to be in sync, with the Transports down 36% from their May 1999 top and the Utilities off 11% from their June 1999 high. Additionally, all three averages are now aligned with the average stock, which has been in a bear market since the advance/decline line peak in April 1998.

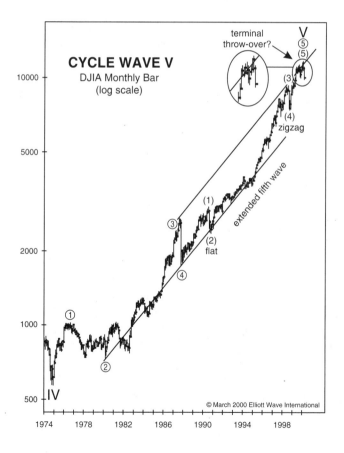

Why I Was Early and What We Have Learned

The Probabilistic Nature of Forecasting Elliott Waves

Nineteen years ago, on January 11, 1982, *The Elliott Wave Theorist* explained both the immense value and the uncertainties that make the Wave Principle, at least to the extent that it is currently understood, immensely useful but only for probabilistic forecasting. See if this communicates to you my view of its value:

In Layman's Terms

Some people have difficulty accepting the idea that the market *always* reflects the Wave Principle since it does not necessarily follow that the Elliott analyst can forecast every single turn with precision. I compare the knowledge of the Wave Principle to having a roadmap of the U.S. when asked the question, "Over exactly what ground will a bus travel if it's making a cross-country trip from New York to L.A.?" Someone without a roadmap, who does not even know that a roadmap exists, will be confronted with a seemingly infinite number of possible paths the bus may take. However, with a map and the knowledge of its function, I can state unequivocally, based on empirical evidence of past occurrence, that the bus will always follow roads, thus eliminating 99.9% of other routes across unpaved land.

Of course, stating, "The bus will always follow roads" is not the same as saying, " I can forecast exactly which roads the bus will take and when it will take them." Yet on precedent, I *can* indicate the *most likely* route from beginning to end. For instance, I would expect a bus to travel interstate highways in preference to U.S. highways and U.S. highways in preference to state highways, etc. At most junctures along the way, I will also know which is the most likely turn, or even when a choice of route has equal possibility. Then there are those exhilarating times when given the route just traveled, I *know* what the next turn will be. Thus, although short of perfection, the Wave Principle does provide a knowledge that often puts the Elliott analyst light-years ahead of most investors.

How can we push these probabilities ever higher in our favor? We can do it by turning every new observation about the action of waves into guidelines that will expand our arsenal of knowledge of how Elliott waves behave.

The manic episode, I think, is finally over. If so, we can sit back and glean some value from the experience so that future Elliotticians analyzing tops of Grand Supercycle degree will have the benefit of precedent, which heretofore was lacking. Let's get down to the cold analytical question: Why did the extent of wave ⑤ cause me such difficulty? More important, what new guidelines can we induce from the market's action to help us in the future?

(1) A Misleading Fifth-Wave Guideline

Fifth waves come in many sizes.

Some fifth waves are so small that, in an event called a truncation, they fail to achieve a new high above the peak prices of wave three and four. For an example, see Figure 1, depicting the 1974-1976 rise. Observe that wave (5) was noticeably small and didn't even make a new high.

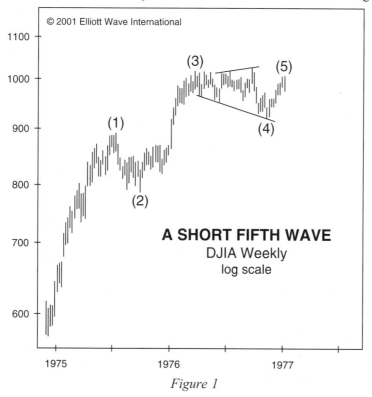

Figure 1

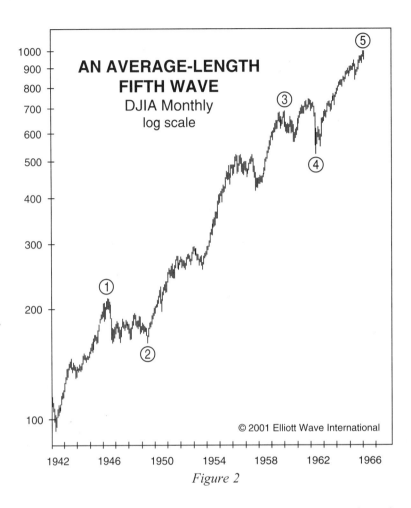

Figure 2

Most fifth waves are of moderate relative length. Elliott formulated a guideline for the length of wave five when wave three is extended. He said that the tendency in such cases was for the fifth wave to be about equal in length to wave one. Figure 2 shows the details of wave III, whose waves ① and ⑤ fit this guideline. This is the guideline that Frost and I used in 1978 and the one I used in 1982 to project the Dow to the 3000-4000 area, a price that would bring wave V to a percentage equivalent with wave I from 1932 to 1937. In making this projection, we thought we were going way out on a limb, and so did the people who dismissed the idea as outrageous. As we know now, that projection ended up being conservative.

A few fifth waves are extended. "Extended" is a specific term referring to an impulse wave that is noticeably longer than the other motive

Figure 3

waves and whose subwaves are more distinct. As Elliott explained, it is normal for *one and only one wave in a sequence* to be extended. Notice in Figure 2 that wave ③ was extended, yet waves ① and ⑤ were not. This is normal wave development.

Figure 3 shows a long fifth wave. The first and third waves in this case were *not* extended, so a long fifth wave was to be expected.

In the 200-year record of aggregate U.S. stock prices, the only major-degree exception to Elliott's single-extension guideline at the time we made our forecast was the 1920s bull market. In all other cases of which I am aware, only one wave of the impulse extended. Since wave III from 1942 to

1966 was already an extension, we concluded that wave V would *not* extend.

Frost and I also projected that wave ⑤ would be the longest wave *within* wave V (see June 1997 commentary in Section One, and the Postscript). That outlook was correct. Ironically, Elliott's single-extension guideline derailed that forecast. The fact that wave ③ from 1980 to 1987 later became extended implied an average-length wave ⑤. At the time, it was a neat package: Both wave ⑤ and wave V would be appropriately non-extended if the Dow were to top in the 3000-4000 range.

As it turned out, wave ⑤ developed an even longer extension than wave ③, creating a double extension within wave V. In that respect, it was just like its cousin in the 1920s, as shown in Figure 4.

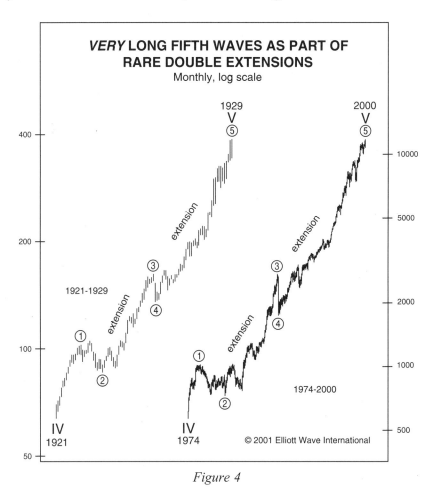

Figure 4

Because wave ⑤ extended, wave V also extended, creating (along with wave III) a double extension within wave (V). Incredibly, then, wave (V) *contained* a double extension and *ended* with a double extension, as you can see in Figure 5. This amazing combination made our original forecast for wave (V)'s termination turn out to be too low. That's how the U.S. market stretched to the greatest overvaluation in the history of stock trading. I had dramatically forecast that the Dow would *quintuple* from its 1982 low. Yet, because of this double double extension, it ended up tripling after that point was reached.

While the Wave Principle was invaluable in recognizing the onset of a great wave V bull market at a time when most investors were cautious and bearish (see Appendix, *Elliott Wave Principle*), Elliott's normally helpful

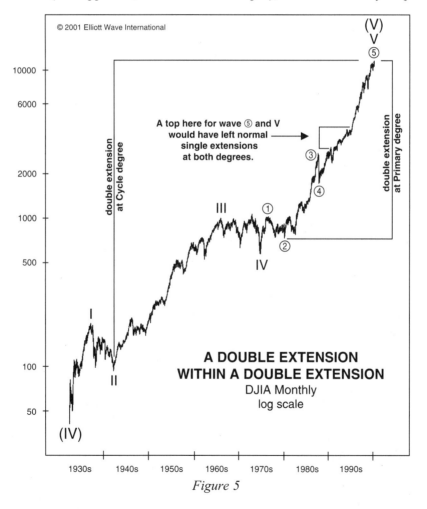

Figure 5

guideline regarding single extensions was in this case an impediment to a successful forecast for the final high.

We can salvage some value from this error in recognizing that we may have discovered a new guideline of wave formation. The fact that wave V exhibited the same relationships as wave V from the 1920s suggests that double extensions, previously thought rare, may be characteristic of fifth waves of Cycle degree and higher in an environment of easy credit, in other words, when stock manias are in force. Figure 4 shows how remarkably these two bull markets tracked each other in terms of form despite the fact that the latter wave V achieved three times the percentage gain in three times the time.

(2) The Guideline of Equality

Elliott's guideline of equality is that when a third wave is extended, the fifth wave tends to be about the same size as the first. On this basis, our wave V was expected to mimic wave I from 1932 to 1937, a 4.716 multiple in just under five years. This is the guideline we used to project a near quintupling for wave V. As a further check on the time element, I studied financial manias of the past and found that they tended to be brief. The tulip mania lasted 3 years; the South Sea Bubble lasted 1 year, culminating an 8-year advance in the stock market; the 1920s boom lasted 8 years. These precedents appeared to support the case for a relatively brief wave V and, later, wave ⑤. Because of the precedent of the 1920s, we pushed the long side of the time aspect of this guideline, projecting an advance of 5 or 8 years from the 1982 low.

As radically bullish as our price and time forecasts were, neither projection proved adequate. From the 1974 low, wave V traveled three times the percentage gain and three times the time of wave I. The seemingly interminable duration is perhaps what threw us off the most. Had the market reached its final destination in 5 or 8 years, we would have been less surprised than we were that it took so long.

What, then, are we to make of Elliott's guideline? Simply stated, it *is* a guideline, not a rule, and the market does not adhere to it when building a double extension. It is nevertheless useful even in such circumstances, because it tells you when you should begin suspecting that a double extension is taking place. As explained in Chapter 4 of *Elliott Wave Principle*, fifth waves adhering to this guideline can equal or have a Fibonacci relationship to wave one. As soon as the percentage gain of wave five exceeds 3/2 of that of wave one, then, an extension in wave five is probably developing, with substantial gains to follow.

(3) A Misleading Channeling Guideline at Supercycle Degree

Normally, an impulse wave stays within a trend channel bound by parallel lines. On rare occasions when it exceeds the upper line, it does so briefly and by a small amount in an event that Elliott called a "throw-over." A throw-over indicates exhaustion.

Naturally, I regarded the channel at Supercycle degree as the most important one (see Figure 6). The Dow was approaching that channel's upper line in 1995, when I released *At the Crest of the Tidal Wave*. It breached that line in 1996 at another reasonable Fibonacci target of 5444, but continued upward to double from there. I really lost my bearings at that point and

Figure 6

did not regain perspective until realizing that the channels at Cycle and Primary degree were directing the price action.

Even the channels at Cycle and Primary degree were somewhat unorthodox. Prices dipped below the lower line in both cases. Nevertheless, connecting the lows of waves two and four and then drawing a parallel line across the top of wave three, as Elliott instructed, generated the correct resistance line for wave five, as you can see on page 157 (from 1996) and the updated Figures 7 and 8. Figure 2-6 of *At the Crest of the Tidal Wave* (1995) had allowed for this picture at Cycle degree, so I knew it was possible. The action around these channels from 1997 to 2000 supplied confidence that I had finally discerned the proper upper boundary for wave ⑤.

Has something like this combination of events happened before? Yes, and at this point, you might be able to guess when it happened.

Figures 9 and 10 show that in the bull market of the 1920s, stock prices soared way above the Supercycle-degree trend channel while nevertheless remaining contained within a parallel channel at Cycle degree, complete with a throw-over at the top. Frost and I showed the Cycle-degree channel of the 1920s in *Elliott Wave Principle* (1978), but at the time, we did not recognize that the resulting breach of the upper channel line at Supercycle degree had significance for the great Cycle wave V bull market that we were forecasting.

Figure 11 shows that in the 1990s, the DJIA also rose significantly above resistance lines at *Grand* Supercycle degree. The higher of those (see dashed line) was met in 1987. The market crashed, re-grouped and then soared right through it. This additional observation leads me to suggest a second new Elliott wave guideline: Breaching an upper channel line may be a rare event generally, but like a double extension, it may be characteristic of fifth waves of Supercycle degree and higher in an environment of easy credit, in other words, when stock manias are in force. It is nevertheless extremely interesting that the parallel channel at one *higher* degree — Submillennium — remains intact.

We now have two new useful Elliott wave guidelines. Two centuries from now, when the next Cycle wave V occurs, this information should come in handy. Please make a note.

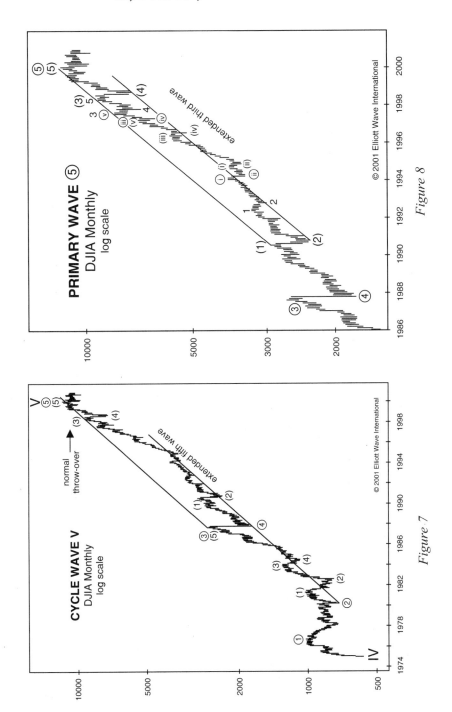

Figure 8

Figure 7

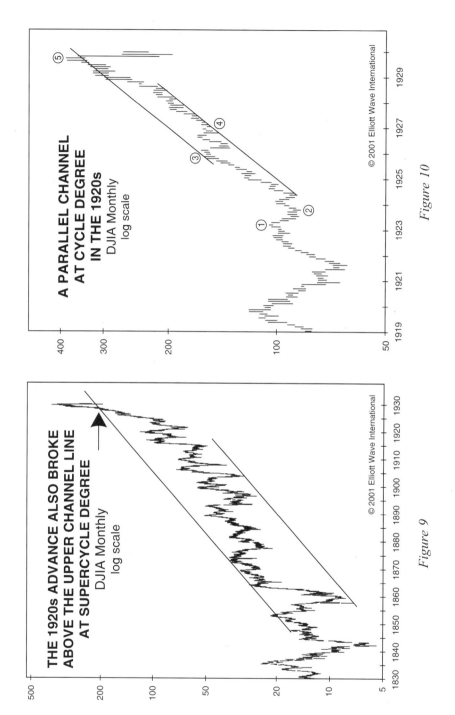

Figure 10

Figure 9

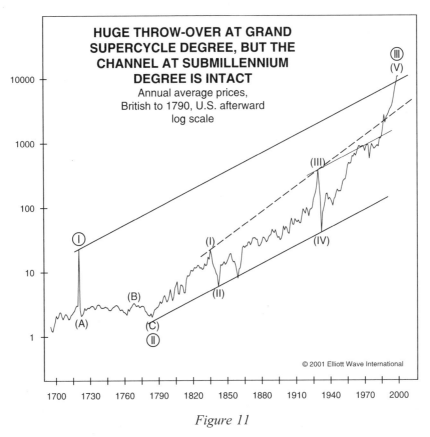

**HUGE THROW-OVER AT GRAND
SUPERCYCLE DEGREE, BUT THE
CHANNEL AT SUBMILLENNIUM
DEGREE IS INTACT**
Annual average prices,
British to 1790, U.S. afterward
log scale

© 2001 Elliott Wave International

Figure 11

(4) Two Starting Points

Complicating the procedure of forecasting was the fact that wave V had (and still has, in some ways) two acceptable starting points: 1974 and 1982. The Appendix of *Elliott Wave Principle* elaborates on this point, and *The Elliott Wave Theorist* referred continually to this duality in ensuing years. Take another look at Figure 6 and observe that the 1974 low met the support line of the Supercycle degree channel perfectly well. From the standpoint of form, then, there was no reason for the Dow to hang around the lower end of the channel for another six years. Yet it did so, even to the point of breaking the line for a couple of days in March 1980 and again for several weeks in the summer of 1982. The first consequence of this tiresome meander is that it made the 1979-1982 period tricky to deal with. Nevertheless, I negotiated it adequately and certainly never lost sight of the fact that a great wave V lay ahead.

The second consequence was more serious. The previous chapter recounts attempts to anticipate wave V's termination point, all of which were exceeded until the 11,889 forecast. Why there were so many projections? There are two main measuring guidelines for projecting the peak price for an impulse: The fifth wave is likely to be a Fibonacci multiple either of wave one or the net travel of waves one through three. Chapter 4 of *Elliott Wave Principle* elaborates on this point. Generally, when other Elliott wave considerations are taken into account, the number of potential targets is quite small. In this case, wave V ignored the single-extension guideline, which expanded the number of available upside targets so that the gain of wave V could have been 1.00, 1.618, 2.618 or 4.236 times the gain of wave I or .382, .618, 1.00 or 1.618 times the net gain of I-III. Even then, there are not as many options as it seems since targets obtained by the two methods often coincide, as in fact they ultimately did. The real problem was that the dual lows of 1974 and 1982 *doubled* the number of upside targets available. Had there been only one acceptable low, which is by far the normal occurrence, there would have been half as many potential targets, and at least on that score during the 1990s, I would have appeared only half as lost. Ultimately, I had to see it to believe that the S&P 500 would become so overpriced that it would yield less than *2/5* of what it did at the top minute in 1929, but that's what it ultimately did.

The chart shown at the top of page 160 shows a measurement used to call a top in the Dow at 8839 in April 1998. That month did mark the all-time high in the Value Line geometric index and the advance-decline line but, of course, not in the Dow. With the Dow at 9200 the following month, a subscriber quickly wrote to apply the same relationship to the 1982 low, projecting 11,889. It was the natural next stop, so *The Elliott Wave Theorist* published it in May 1998 (see the December 3, 1999 commentary in Section Two*)*, which turned out to be the last one we needed. It was a simple relationship. Using the 1982 low, wave V = .618 x I–III in percentage terms. It was so simple that had the degree of wave V been of Intermediate degree or smaller, this target would have appeared entirely reasonable from the start.

It is not clear to me even today whether the *particular* relationship that finally produced the price and timing of the ultimate peak should have been the primary original forecast. We have virtually no data on Grand Super-cycle peaks, the only one on record being the top of the South Sea Bubble in 1720. The last Supercycle peak, in 1929, occurred after eight years' advance in wave V and gave no hint that the next wave V would last 18 years from 1982 and 26 years from 1974. From preliminary work on Fibonacci relationships among the waves in the Supercycle, I believe that the market has accommodated both of those lows in creating its intricate structure. I am completing a book on that subject (tentatively titled *Beautiful Pictures*) that I hope will demonstrate this point. So while the dual lows make for interesting study, they immensely frustrated real-time application.

(5) The Post-Triangle Thrust Guideline

Elliott stated that a triangle correction in the "wave four" position typically leads to "a short, sharp thrust" to a new high, constituting all of wave five. You can see Elliott's guideline at work in Figure 1, which shows an expanding triangle in the wave (4) position. It was followed be a short, sharp thrust, so short in fact that it didn't even make a new high. As you can see in Figure 6, wave IV from 1966 to 1974 was also an expanding triangle. Right off the bat, then, Elliott's triangle guideline, normally so reliable, indicated a short wave V.

Frost and I took this guideline seriously in *Elliott Wave Principle* to the point of considering a diagonal triangle pattern for wave V, which we nevertheless dismissed in favor of a rise all the way up to the upper parallel of the channel at Supercycle degree. We were pushing the envelope in doing so, and yet the market ultimately went way beyond our elevated target. This guideline was *really* misleading. After observing similar results many times in commodities, I believe we have another amendment to Elliott's guidelines: If prices continue past the normal "thrust" target after a triangle, they are likely to continue *way* beyond it to make wave five the longest of the entire sequence.

(6) The Skewing of Waves in a Mania

During the mania following the 1987 crash, impulses were stretched upward and corrections were shallow, with their "C" waves ending at higher levels than their "A" waves, creating dramatically skewed "running" flats and triangles (see *Elliott Wave Principle*, Figures 1-38, 1-39 and 1-43). I was in fact poised to turn bullish three times: in late 1988, late 1990 and again in late 1994. Each time, I expected a "C" wave that would take out the previous low, as would be normal in a zigzag or flat. It would have made for a great opportunity to get back on track. In each case, the Dow held above the previous bottom and turned up without me. Figure 12 shows

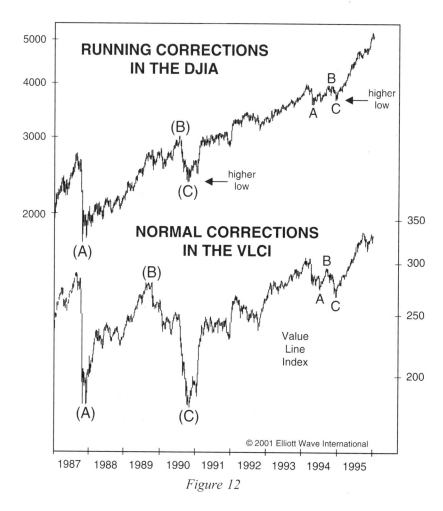

Figure 12

two of those instances, along with charts of the Value Line Composite Index to show that a C-wave influence was hidden in other areas of the market. Here's how *The Elliott Wave Theorist* stated the problem in the May 29, 1997 issue:

> The mania has influenced waves to deviate far more than normal from textbook forms. For example, in a normal bull market, the period from 1987 to 1990 would have been a major correction subdividing A-B-C. As you can see by the chart, the Value Line Index had this profile, while the Dow did not. Similarly, the period from May 1996 to April 1997 would have been a large correction, also subdividing A-B-C. As you can see [in Figure 13], the AMEX index had this profile. The

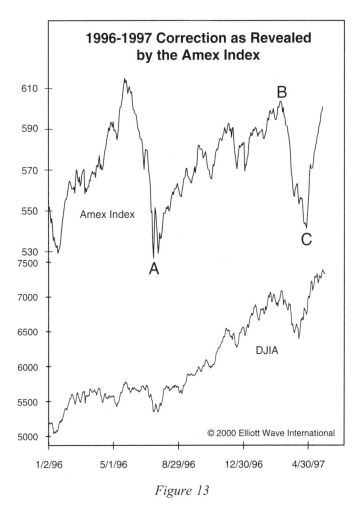

Figure 13

NASDAQ (not shown) reflected these forces to a degree, but the averages dominated by blue chips show barely a hint of them, which is why wave analysis on those indexes has been so difficult. In our latter example, the "C" wave failed to exceed the low of the "A" wave, which is about the maximum extent of wave interpretation difficulty in a normal bull market. Manias themselves are predictable, as EWT's 1983 description demonstrates. However, the movements within a mania are so powerfully skewed upward that determining where you are *within* the wave is a challenge, to say the least. After the top, the same thing will happen on the downside. Our advantage then will be a monopoly on that very perspective.

That last sentiment is worth remembering as the market prepares to head lower in the Grand Supercycle bear.

Assessment

So as you can see, during the 1990s, I had to deal with a broken Supercycle trend channel, an unheard-of double-double extension, a record breaking exception to Elliott's guideline for fifth waves following triangles, an inapplicable guideline of first and fifth wave equality, two starting points for wave V and numerous shallow and upwardly skewed corrections. I hope you can see why the resulting analytical challenge was difficult, to say the least.

This situation was frustrating because *I did not make any mistakes in applying Elliott's guidelines, nor are the guidelines wrong.* Guidelines are not the same as the *rules* of wave formation, which is why they are called by a different name. Chapter 1 of *Elliott Wave Principle* makes this point:

> Elliott noted the important fact that each pattern has identifiable *requirements* as well as *tendencies.* From these observations, he was able to formulate numerous rules and guidelines for proper wave identification.

By definition, tendencies apply *usually*, not always. Normally, variances are not a problem because other guidelines provide the necessary clues. This case was different.

I can now state precisely what happened: The 1974-2000 wave V was a rare market situation in which prices failed to adhere to *multiple* normally reliable guidelines, simultaneously and repeatedly. For an Elliott analyst with historical knowledge limited to 100 years of reliable data (and another 200 years of possibly reliable data) from which to generalize about wave formation, that environment was akin to being caught in a maze of funhouse mirrors, where reality is seemingly distorted.

Obviously, though, reality was *not* distorted. This is apparently the way that the market can behave when finishing a wave of Supercycle or Grand Supercycle degree. At the time, we just did not have enough examples on the record to modify the guidelines accordingly. Now, we do. Because of this unfortunate episode, we have formulated some important correcting nuances in several of Elliott's guidelines for wave interpretation, summarized as follows:

(1) When waves above Cycle degree are culminating, sometimes the largest applicable trend channel fails to contain prices on the upside, in which case they will adhere to a channel at one lesser degree.

(2) Fifth waves of major degree are prone to containing a double extension, in subwaves three and five.

(3) If a fifth wave following a triangle does not stop at a normal thrust measurement, it is likely to be an especially long extension.

(4) If a fifth wave following an extended third wave is not roughly equal in percentage gain to wave one (at least within a 3/2 multiple), then wave five is probably a developing extension with much further to go.

(5) In the second extension of a double extension, corrections will be exceptionally shallow and may appear as running flats or triangles.

With these amendments in mind, Elliotticians of the future should be able to avoid a prematurely bearish stance within Cycle and Supercycle degree fifth waves. I hope this book survives long enough to be of service to them!

Fortunately, we have three examples of bear markets of Supercycle degree (1835-1859 and 1929-1932) and larger (1720-1784) on the record, so we should be prepared for what lies ahead. For more on this theme, see Chapter 5 of *At the Crest of the Tidal Wave*.

In retrospect, I can see many ways that I could have handled the period better so as to have stayed with the trend longer. On the other hand, everything is easy in retrospect. It's the future that's always such a pesky challenge. I did decide that *The Elliott Wave Theorist*'s monthly publishing schedule was an artificial impediment to patience, which I have now rectified by commenting on the market only when its wave pattern prompts a response. So far, it has suited my temperament much better.

Nevertheless, in some market environments, you can't be both prudent and right. Anyone who was happily invested in the late 1990s mania was, almost by definition, oblivious to the immense technical negatives and will undoubtedly hold on throughout the bear market that will devastate so many portfolios. We kept our bull market profits and will have our capital intact when the bottom arrives.

POSTSCRIPT

March 2001 issue
(interview conducted February 2001)

Robert Prechter is Bearish. He remains aggressively bearish on the stock market long term, though dramatic rallies will occur along the way. Near term, his firm is forecasting a tradable turn on March 8/9 and another one on March 22/23.

The Elliott Wave Theorist/Financial Forecast

Robert Prechter has been publishing *The Elliott Wave Theorist* since 1979. In the 1980s, Bob was #1 several times in *Timer Digest* and usually in the Top Ten, sometimes in all three markets. Twice he made our cover.

Being right on the slipping S&P index lately has helped boost the Elliott wave services into our current Top Ten list for stocks. Bob thinks the selling is far from over. "Are you kidding?" he asks. "The market is still in its top formation. It's hardly gotten going yet."

Few people recall that Bob's first book with A.J. Frost, *Elliott Wave Principle,* published in 1978, was perhaps the most bullish book of its time. In 1982, the *Theorist* called for a Dow run to nearly 4000 back when it was in the 800s. "In 1983, I used the term *mania* to describe what was coming. As it turns out, it was even bigger than I originally thought."

In recent years, Prechter and his staff have gotten a reputation as the biggest bears on Wall Street. "We were bearish way too soon. But we never let up because we know how historic this top is." With the NASDAQ already down 60% and many high flyers facing bankruptcy, some people are wishing they had paid some attention to the Elliott wave guys back in 1998 when the advance-decline line topped out along with the average stock. "The main thing we tried to do in the final years of the frenzy was to keep people from saddling up to go over the cliff."

That kind of long-term perspective has served Bob well in gold, where he stayed steadfastly bearish while calling for rallies along the way. It has kept the Elliott-wave service in our Top Five list fairly often during gold's long bear market.

The Elliott Wave Team

Due to the modern wonder of cloning, Bob is now three people. Though he still writes *The Elliott Wave Theorist,* his associates Steve Hochberg and Pete Kendall write the *Financial Forecast* and the *Short Term Update,* and then Bob edits it. "These guys are great," says Bob. "I looked for a long time to find people who could actually improve our services, and they've done that. If anything, Steve goes overboard taking care of our *Update* subscribers. And analysis on market psychology and social trends doesn't get better than Pete's." If Bob sounds happy, it's because subscription totals are the highest they've been since his name was a household word back in the '80s.

"You need new blood to keep things fresh, and these guys have it," says Bob. This arrangement gives Bob more time to revive some of the classic studies from his early days. "I forgot how much original research I was doing back before I started running a company," he says.

In the 1990s, Bob expanded his operation to generate analysis for institutions. His firm, Elliott Wave International, now provides round-the-clock analysis on all major stock indexes, currencies and interest rates worldwide. "I located the best and brought them here," says Bob. "You should see how well these guys call markets, all day long and all through the year."

You can still get the *Financial Forecast* for the same price as always. Its companion service, the *Short Term Update,* issues a detailed analysis every Monday, Wednesday and Friday to keep subscribers on top of the scenario forecast in the monthly letter. Most of the insights from Elliott Wave International are not available anywhere else because their approach to the market, which is based on price patterns, is unique.

The Elliott wave contingent is certainly in the minority, but it's often good to weigh the arguments of those saying something different from the crowd. You can check out EWI at their web site, which Prechter is proud of. "It's the biggest technical analysis website on the Internet," he says. "We have a free Elliott wave course, a bulletin board, a 'bears' den,' daily market commentary, great books, pay-per-view special reports (there's one called *Stocks and Sex)* and a club with all kinds of free benefits. We do chats with Steve and even video updates and interviews on the markets." *Video* updates? "Yep, we're on the cutting edge of everything on the web."

Timer Digest has been following *The Elliott Wave Theorist* since June 1984, and it currently ranks number 4 for three months, number 4 for six

months and number 9 for the most recent 52 weeks. It also ranks number 1
for Gold and number 6 for the Long Term.

Taking Advantage of Trends

It is common knowledge that bear markets move two or three times as
fast as bull markets, but few investors and traders make money in them.
Bob sees this as novice psychology. "It's the same market. Don't you want
to be on the right side regardless of direction? *Particularly* when your gains
pile up at triple the rate?"

The Elliott wave team thinks stocks will be in a bear market for at
least four years, with the biggest drops coming in 2002, 2003 and maybe
2004 as well. How low will they go? "Well, first of all, the NASDAQ will
be back in triple digits before you know it. Also, the S&P and the Dow are
going to go a lot lower than anyone imagines." Of course, there will be
some convincing bear market rallies along the way and maybe even a new
high in some narrow index. "Rallies are great for adding to shorts, but you
have to let them play out first." The boys are also gearing up for another
possible sharp gold rally.

"I know our opinion sounds radical," says Prechter, "but I've been
hearing that as long as I've been following the markets. I heard it back in
1982 about my bullishness on the Dow. I heard it again when I turned
super-bearish on gold at $710."

Prechter berates the myth that bulls are always good guys. "Today's
bulls are nobody's friend. They are enticing their followers to take huge
risks with hard-earned money, and they will not be answerable when these
folks lose it."

Long Term Forecast Still in Progress

Below is a picture of the DJIA as of 1978, when *Business Week* was reporting as follows:
— "More and more economists are forecasting recession."[1]
— "If the dollar continues to plummet, the pressure may prove unstoppable."[2]
— "The mood of the consumer and of business executives indicate a deterioration in expectations about prospective business conditions."[3]
— "The public's...fear of inflation has never been greater than it is today."[4]

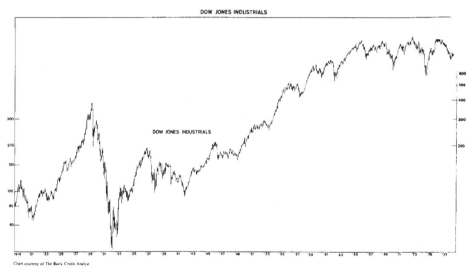

DOW JONES INDUSTRIALS

Figure 1

What would *you* have forecast for the stock market at that time?

In 1978, the book *Elliott Wave Principle* depicted what we thought would be a reasonable shape for wave V and its aftermath, reproduced in Figure 2. It was derived by inverting the 1929-1937 period and adding it to the low that had just occurred in March of that year. Our graph called for the DJIA to climb from the 1974 low in "five Primary waves with the fifth

Forecast from *Elliott Wave Principle* (1978)

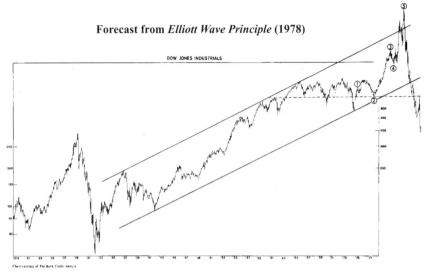

Figure 2

Figure 3

extending," carrying beyond the upper trendline of the channel at Super-cycle degree, and then to fall below 400. This forecast and the quote on page 4 of this book show that we knew back in those early days the wild experience that lay ahead. The first half of that forecast took longer and went higher than anticipated (see Figure 3), but otherwise, this picture was a darn good guide to the future. The rising portion of the projection appears to be finished. Now it remains to be seen whether the second half comes to pass. If you want to know what happens next, the descriptions in *At the Crest* remain as pertinent as ever.

NOTES:

[1] *Business Week.* (1978, March 8). "The Talk Grows of a Coming Recession."

[2] *Business Week.* (1978, March 20). "The Dollar Fades as a Reserve Currency."

[3] *Business Week.* (1978, May 8). "Business Outlook."

[4] *Business Week.* (1978, May 22.) "How Inflation Threatens the Fabric of U.S. Society."